CONTROL

why the health and social care system
need not have failed my mother

For Mum and Aunty Ann

two sisters who passed away within seven weeks of each other in two different hospitals in two different counties

I love you
I miss you

BEYOND MY CONTROL

why the health and social care system
need not have failed my mother

Suzan Collins

BOOKS

Hammersmith Health Books
London, UK

First published in 2013 by Hammersmith Health Books – an imprint of
Hammersmith Books Limited
14 Greville Street, London EC1N 8SB, UK
www.hammersmithbooks.co.uk

Disclaimer
This is a true story of the experiences and recollections of the author but
she has changed some names to protect the privacy of the individuals
concerned. The story is entirely from the author's subjective perspective
and she acknowledges that her interpretation of the behaviour of others
may not match entirely with their own recollection of events.
The author has omitted the names of hospitals and care services so that
her book can focus on general issues with caring for vulnerable people;
it is not intended to be a criticism of any particular service. Her intention
is to show what poor practice is, how it can affect those on the receiving
end, and how practice might improve.
Whilst the advice and information in this book are believed to be true and
accurate at the date of going to press, neither the author nor the publisher
can accept any legal responsibility or liability for any errors or omissions
that may have been made.

British Library Cataloguing in Publication Data: A CIP record of this book
is available from the British Library.

ISBN (print edition): 978-1-78161-028-2
ISBN (ebook): 978-1-78161-029-9

Commissioning editor: Georgina Bentliff
Designed and typeset by: Julie Bennett
Production: Helen Whitehorn, Pathmedia
Printed and bound by TJ International Ltd
Cover photograph: Shutterstock © Viktor Gladkov

Contents

Acknowledgements

I should like to thank the following people for their support in writing this book:

Shonagh Methven, Jane Cassell, Penny Mayhew and Rebeccah Giltrow. I should also like to thank my brother, sister, niece and cousins, for their love and support. Also Tim, for being there. And I should like to thank my Editor, Georgina Bentliff, for taking on this project.

On the following pages I have included quotations from other copyright works, with permission:

- Page 23 – Judy Waterlow
- Page 88 – 'Red' as sung by Daniel Merriweather. Words and music by Scott McFarnon, Amanda Ghost and Ian Dench © 2007, reproduced by permission of Red Ink Music Publishing, EMI Music Publishing Ltd and Kobalt Music Publishing Ltd.
- Page 150 – quotation from Dame Cicely Saunders
- 'One at Rest' – I have not been able to find out who the author of this poem is. Please contact me at the publishers if you know

About the Author

Suzan Collins is a professional trainer and consultant in health and social care, working across the country. She assesses staff performance in Health, Social Care and Management, delivers training, carries out pre-inspection (Care Quality Commission) compliance checks and advises on policies and procedures on subjects that include 'safeguarding' vulnerable people from harm and abuse. Suzan campaigns for better standards of health and social care in care/nursing homes, at home and in hospitals. She also campaigns for better support for staff providing this care. In addition, she is the author of six, internationally selling open-learning workbooks, one of which is on Safeguarding Adults.

SPC Consultancy & Training
Specialising in social care and management throughout England, in line with the Health and Social Care Act and Care Quality Commission Regulations.
Website: www.spcconsultancy.com
Facebook: https://www.facebook.com/pages/SPC-Consultancy-Training-Suzan-Collins/146096555424838
Twitter: @suzancollins
Blog: http://suzancollins.wordpress.com/

Preface

I have worked in the care sector for 33 years, and, until the events recorded in this book took place, had always taken it for granted that everyone providing care for vulnerable people really did just that – they *cared*. This work demands high levels of responsibility and is not highly paid, but it can be hugely rewarding in that you can make a real difference to people's lives. That that difference can be for ill as well as for good was only truly brought home to me by my own mother's tragic experience.

There was an accident with a hoist, I was told, at my mother's nursing home. She had to be admitted to hospital with fractures. What should have been a straightforward trip to hospital and back to the nursing home did not happen. My mother was never to leave the hospital alive and finding out what had really happened was to take me over two years.

My 'day' job is to provide training in health and social care management, consultancy and auditing of services yet the poor and uncaring practices that my family and I encountered at the hospital and nursing home left me aghast. I was astonished at the way older people, including my mother, were treated. I have been equally astonished and concerned since to find how few people know what constitutes good practice and that they can challenge professionals if they have concerns.

Beyond My Control tells the story of my mother's ordeal and the efforts I and my family made to put things right. It is also intended to show what good and poor practices are, and what to do when things go wrong.

It is the story of particular events, but with a general message. For that reason I have purposely not said which home or hospital was responsible and do not wish in any way to focus on specific organisations. That would be to miss the point of this book, which is to raise awareness of the dangers faced by all people in care if that care is inadequate. I have also provided practical advice at the end of many of the chapters and in an appendix at the end of the book to show what you, the reader, can do to stop something this bad happening to you.

It is particularly hard to be on the receiving end of poor care when you are an 'insider', and the guilt you feel in not being able to stop bad things happening is magnified. I have discussed this with many other health and social care professionals. They have felt, as I did, the pressure of their family's (and their own) expectation that they would be able to sort everything out. Coming to terms with what you may regard at the time as 'failure' can take years.

There are a lot of brilliant staff out there, doing a great job. It is a minority of poor managers and uncaring individuals who let both their colleagues and the people they care for down. I hope any social care and health care professionals who read this book will feel encouraged both to provide the best care they can and to raise the alarm when they see things that do not seem right. We all share that responsibility – not to turn a blind eye.

Introduction

I have over 30 years' experience of working in the four care sectors: NHS, social services, voluntary and private. For many of these years I successfully commissioned and managed residential services, supporting people with learning disabilities and behaviours that were challenging due to communication difficulties. I have always tried to raise standards for people receiving care, and to promote dignity and an awareness of the needs and rights of vulnerable people. And of the staff who do the caring.

In my current role as a freelance trainer, consultant and auditor of services in social care and management, I deliver training, carry out external audits of services and advise on policies and procedures on subjects that include 'safeguarding'. Safeguarding covers an understanding of what constitutes poor practice, harm and abuse, how to protect vulnerable people from abuse and poor practices, and what to do if you suspect abuse or poor practices. As I have carried out this role across the country, I have seen many examples of good practice, but I have also uncovered poor practices and outright direct or indirect abuse. Some staff who have told me of their concerns have been happy to go back to their workplace and discuss their concerns with their managers; others have not. Either way, I have always told participants at the beginning of a training session that 'everything is confidential here today unless it goes outside the boundary, and then I have to report it.' Going outside the boundary would, for example, be learning that an individual at a home is at risk.

I also worked with various NVQ companies across the country for some years, until NVQs changed to the Diploma system. This involved going into residential homes and day centres (known collectively as 'services') to assess staff and managers who support people with learning disabilities and older people. My role was to observe and assess the performance of NVQ candidates against a set of standards, and suggest ideas if required; for example, the use of different formats of communication with one individual, talking more slowly to another, promoting choice and using risk assessments. I could always tell if staff had genuinely taken my recommendations on board as I assessed them over a period of time, and sometimes I visited to assess other staff, so those I had previously observed and assessed were not always aware of my presence. As a previous manager of residential homes, I am practised in observing individual performance while reviewing other aspects of a service. Many of the older people's services I have visited in this way have been graded as excellent by the Care Quality Commission (I will come back to them later). However, as you will see, as well as seeing some very good practices, I have also seen some very disturbing ones.

Given my experience, you would think I would know just what to do when faced with poor care for my own family, but knowledge and power are two very different things; I was to discover that knowing what good practice should be did not mean I could get it for my mother.

Ironically, I was delivering training in good practice when I received a telephone call to say that my 77-year-old mother had been injured in an accident at her nursing home. We were told the injury had occurred while she was being hoisted on to her bed.

'Accidents happen,' my sister said.

'No, they don't!' I replied. 'Accidents don't happen. If you're using equipment, such as a hoist, correctly then accidents don't happen.'

Within a few days, my mother was back in hospital with another fracture, yet nobody but our family seemed to think this was a cause for concern. Very sadly this was the start of a chain of avoidable but calamitous happenings. As a family we struggled to change the course events were taking, but as you will read, the weight of 'the system' was against us.

This book is about my personal experiences as both a professional and a daughter. Not only does it explain what happened – or, in some cases, what we think happened – it also sets out to tell those on the receiving end of social and health care what standards they can and should expect and to remind professional carers, support workers, homes managers and nurses and doctors, what is acceptable practice and what is not.

Beyond My Control tells the true story of the poor practice and neglectful hospital treatment experienced by my mother, and my own efforts to investigate how and why this happened – and to stop it happening to anyone else in the future. To highlight what I knew to be good practice and the standard of care that my mother should have received I have also included incidents from my working life, assessing staff performance for NVQ qualifications and holding workshops and other training events for staff working in care services.

I hope this book will raise awareness of standards and the importance of not accepting low ones. We need to do more to ensure vulnerable people receive the respect and care they deserve. It is my intention through this book to enable people to do exactly that – recognise good and poor practice and know what they can do to put things right.

Something I must say from the outset is, you should give praise, thanks and appreciation to staff when they do do things right. Many may do things well but never get thanked; after a while they may not work as well as they once did, and standards deteriorate.

And when things go wrong, it is very often a training or lack of support issue. Working across the country, I have seen the effects of training for staff supporting older people being too limited. In other places, too much training has overwhelmed staff, who find they can't take in what they have been taught. They may also have had to come in on their day off to attend training. It is not surprising they may then feel resentful and not value training if they have been working long hours, on their feet for most of the time.

Despite the events I describe here, I continue to deliver training throughout the UK and to provide a consultancy service. A new focus, thanks to my personal experience, is to help organisations to handle complaints and to review complaints procedures. My mother has left me with a mission to improve care for all vulnerable people and I hope to impart the importance of that mission to all my readers. Whether you and your loved ones have experienced anything like this yourselves, I hope you will join me in saying 'Never again!'

Chapter 1

Accidents don't happen

It was 11 March when my sister called; our mother had a broken ankle due to an accident with the hoist in her nursing home.

'Accidents happen,' my sister said.

'No, they don't!' I replied. 'Accidents don't happen. If you're using equipment, like the hoist, correctly then accidents do *not* happen.'

Mum's leg and ankle had been put in plaster and she had been returned from the hospital to the nursing home. Our brother, Keith, would be able to visit today, but Ann, my sister, couldn't get time off work. I told her I would sort my work out, take a few days off and go down to see Mum. I didn't tell her about the serious concerns that I, in my professional role as a trainer, had been having about services in the past few weeks. She didn't need to know that.

I was able to go down to the West Country the following week – a seven-hour journey from my home on the east coast on five different trains. But I couldn't rearrange the current week's workload; it was too short notice and I didn't want to let people down; I knew how difficult it was for managers to take staff off the rota to attend training and back-fill it with other staff, or even agency staff. This was a personal and professional dilemma for me as I did not want to let my mother down either, but I knew that my brother and the staff from the nursing home would look after her. Mum had had a back injury when she was younger and as the years had gone on the problems with her spine had worsened, causing difficulty with walking; she needed help with manoeuvring and personal care. Now she could not bear any weight on her legs and had to be moved using a hoist. In her 40s Mum had been diagnosed with type 2 diabetes which was controlled by a healthy diet and tablets. In all other respects she was in reasonable health, or had been until this accident.

Putting worries about Mum to one side, I kept my appointment with the manager of a service (the general term we use for care homes and other services) to discuss what training she wanted. I was surprised at how warm and homely the service was and how friendly, welcoming and happy the staff seemed, despite being very busy wheeling people in wheelchairs or hoisting them or supporting their arms whilst they walked to the dining room. They conversed with the individuals they were helping, but it was 'talk as we go'; there was little time to sit and chat. I noted some staff calling the individuals 'love' or 'darling'; I regard this as disrespectful because it implies it is too much trouble to remember names. I hoped these staff members would be on the training course so I could address such issues with them. I was told the morning shifts were the busiest and, as I left the service, I hoped the afternoon shift would be quieter and more relaxing, allowing the staff to spend quality time with the individuals they were caring for.

'Wheelchairs are only for transferring,' I heard the manager tell a staff member as we walked through the service, 'Not for sitting in for long periods of time, as that can cause pressure sores.'

I held the training session on Dignity in Care for Older People and we worked through what are called the 'person-centred values', a set of principles that all staff should adhere to. They are

Privacy, Choice, Respect, Independence, Individuality, Identity, Dignity and Rights. I asked for examples from the staff on how they promoted these values. Some of the values they found easy to tackle. For example, for Privacy, they came up with 'Close the toilet door; put a towel over the lap whilst the individual is on the toilet; close the bedroom door; knock on the door and wait for a response.' I added: 'It's important not to go into the bedroom if the individual isn't in there and hasn't given you permission to go inside – privacy is a basic human need and everyone has a right to it.'

When it came to Respect they got a little stuck. I gave them a hand-out to go through and this gave me the opportunity to say 'You need to call the people you support by their preferred name. If there is a new individual in the service and his records say "Mr Terry Smith", don't automatically call him Terry. Ask him what he likes to be called. He may say he likes to be called Mr Smith; if he does, make a note of this so all staff will call him that.' Some of the staff looked a bit sheepish. 'Many of the people you support won't like you calling them "darling", "love" and "lovey". Why do you use these terms?' In response I heard mumbling of 'it's easier'. We talked through this and staff could see how patronising or disrespectful this can be.

Then we came to the issue of respecting individuals' faiths. They stared at me as though I had said something wrong or something they have never heard of before.

'Are there people living at the home with different religions?' I asked.

'Some,' came the reply.

'Are the individuals in the service offered the opportunity to go to church – or another place of worship – if they want to?'

'Some are.'

'Why only some?' I probed.

'We haven't got enough staff for all of them who want to go to church.'

'I know it can be difficult because there are a lot of people living in the home and some need a lot of support. Have you thought of how they can attend church without taking the staff from the home?' I asked. They gave me a blank stare.

'You could discuss with your manager about using volunteers, or people from the church who are willing to pick one or two up in their cars and take them. How many people used to go to church independently before they moved into the home?'

The staff went through the individuals and found quite a few who used to go independently. I then questioned how many of these people were still able to go to church independently or would be if a lift was available. The staff were amazed when they realised that this was possible for quite a few. I advised them to discuss it with their manager, who might need to devise a risk assessment to ensure their safety.

As always when I do these sessions, Dignity prompted some interesting responses. I told them, 'Some organisations have a policy to say that only same-sex staff will support individuals with their personal care. What about,' I asked 'the preferences of British white females?' As I expected, this was greeted by a lot of blank stares. Someone said, 'White females don't have any culture so they don't have any preferences'. This answer is no longer the shock to me it once was. Other trainers make culture an issue, but forget that the 'default' white British person also has a culture, just not a minority one. I told them, 'White women have preferences too and you must ask them who they want to support them with their personal care.'

Then I asked, 'How about making sure personal care is carried out discreetly to avoid humiliation and embarrassment? That means, for instance, not shouting out to colleagues that you're now going to take Mrs Smith to the toilet.'

'Oh dear! We do that sometimes,' said one staff member and others smirked. 'Okay, let's do a simulation exercise,' I told them. 'Split into groups of three: one is a resident and two are staff.

One "member of staff" stand some distance apart from the two. The "staff member" with the "resident", shout to the second "member of staff" that you're taking the "resident" to the toilet. Take it in turns for you all to be the individual receiving support. And then come back to here and tell us how it felt.'

And they did.

'I felt so small.'

'I was embarrassed.'

'I didn't like it.'

'No one needs to know that I'm being taken to the toilet.'

'The staff need to know so they don't ask that individual again, but they can see with their eyes that a staff member is taking someone to the toilet,' I told them. 'Was that a useful exercise?' I got a big 'Yes!' in response.

When we came to Choice and Rights we had another interesting discussion.

'What would you do if an individual who is a wheelchair user wanted to go swimming?' I asked them.

'They wouldn't be able to go if they're in a wheelchair, would they?'

I raised my eyebrows and looked at their faces, indicating that I was waiting for someone to respond to what had just been said, but an answer did not come.

'Why not?' I asked.

'How would we get the chair to the swimming pool, and how would the individual get in the pool?' one asked, with attitude.

'Black cabs take wheelchairs as do some other taxi firms. So the individual can get to the pool. How does he or she get into the pool?' I asked.

'The individual can't because they can't walk,' said a staff member slumped in a chair.

'What you could do is find a pool that has facilities to help people get into the pool. For example, pools have hoists and slings. You may need to ring in advance for them to get the equipment out. What do you do if you ring a sports centre and they haven't got a hoist?'

'Ring another one,' said the staff member, who was no longer slumped in her chair.

'Yes, that's right. You also need to encourage the individuals to inform the pool that they're discriminating if they have no facilities for wheelchair users to get into the pool. If the resident can't or doesn't feel comfortable doing this, you can do this on their behalf.'

I went onto the subject of beliefs and asked for examples; the room fell silent. I told them that many of our beliefs come from our past – from family, friends, TV, colleagues, the way we were brought up, religious experiences, education and life experiences. I split them into small groups to discuss how their parents' and grandparents' lives had differed from theirs. They appeared to enjoy this and I asked them how their discussions related to the older people they supported.

'My granddad says I should be grateful to have a lovely bath in the bathroom as he had to have a bath in a steel tub in front of the fire,' said one staff member.

'Yeah, my mum only had a bath once a week when she was younger.'

'My granddad changes his underwear every day but still only changes his shirt and trousers once a week,' added another.

We talked about how they themselves showered once or twice a day, but how this might be a very different habit from those that the individuals they support might be used to.

'Some of the individuals don't like having showers,' said one staff member and others agreed.

'If they clearly show they don't like having a shower, why can't they have a bath instead?' I asked.

'Takes too long,' came a reply.

'How must that feel for the individual, who more than likely has never had a shower, but now has to have them?' I looked at their faces and they silently agreed with me that this was wrong. I told them I would discuss it with the manager afterwards.

At tea break I could hear staff talking about what they had learnt and it confirmed to me that this was a worthwhile course for them. They talked about how they provided privacy and choice for some individuals and how they would now offer choice and independence to others. They were buzzing with ideas.

After the break we did some practical exercises. They were embarrassed at first, but then enjoyed learning from the tasks of feeding someone and changing an incontinence pad. They did these tasks with each other, asked for feedback from the person they had fed and changed and then swapped roles. Feedback included that they didn't like yogurt dribbling onto their chin and they felt like a baby when the staff used the spoon to scoop it up and attempt to put it back into their mouth.

'What could you have done?' I asked. There was silence.

'Use a napkin,' I told them.

I wondered if the staff at my mother's home were like these staff and, if so, did they have access to this type of training? I shuddered at the thought that they might not. Fortunately my mother did not need help with eating, but she did need help with going to the toilet.

'I really didn't know how embarrassing it was to have people in between your legs and putting a pad on,' said one staff member.

'I didn't mind being fed, but I didn't like how the staff put the spoon to my mouth expecting me to open it without being asked. She didn't even ask if I wanted another mouthful. How bad is that?' asked another.

'Remember, this is only role play today, but it's good that you've experienced these things and know how it feels for the people you support,' I told them.

At the end of the session I heard a difference in the staff, a more upbeat confidence as to what is right and what is wrong. Feeling good about how the day had gone I turned on my mobile phone and found a text from a number I didn't recognise.

'Sorry to bother you. I've been given your number to ask for some advice. I want to do some activities with a resident with dementia but the manager says "she is too far gone" – her words not mine. Please help. I don't know what to do.'

My thoughts went to my mother, hoping that she had not been written off like this in her nursing home, not that she had any mental problems. I gave some advice and told the staff member to get back to me if she needed any more. I was pleased for her that she didn't.

Later that evening I was about to jump in the bath when my mobile rang. I looked at the caller display, hoping it was someone who wouldn't mind me calling them back later, but it was a number I didn't recognise, so I answered it. It was a staff member from my training course.

'I didn't want to say in the class but we have a resident with serious dementia, and when it gets really bad she is very distraught and she shouts that she wants to die.'

'I'm really sorry to hear that,' I said and continued, after a silence at the other end. 'It must be very difficult for the individuals in the service, and for you.'

'And for her husband who comes to visit her. She doesn't recognise him. I don't understand dementia so I can't help her. It's all so sad.'

'Dementia can bring two losses to loved ones,' I told her. 'One loss is the person to dementia and the second loss is the person who has dementia to...' and before I could carry on, the staff member said, 'Death'.

'Have you been in post long?' I asked. 'Is your name down on the training list to attend a course on dementia?'

She answered 'No' to both questions and I advised her

to discuss it with her manager and ask to be put on a course because it is very important for staff to be trained in the subject before working with people with dementia. It's a specialist area and needs staff with the right attitude, as do all care jobs.

I was often asked for advice and if it was not possible to talk, I would suggest what to do by text, including reporting concerns to the manager or, if the manager was involved, to the Care Quality Commission. The following afternoon I rang a service to speak to one of my NVQ candidates. Another of my candidates, Layla, answered. Layla was about to come off shift, then take an individual into town in her own time – something that some staff do as there is not enough time available while on shift to do it. I hoped the manager was offering my candidate some time off in lieu, but from her response that didn't sound very likely.

Debbie, the candidate I had rung for, was off sick with stress. I was told she had accidentally hurt an individual she was supporting with her newly applied false nails – something many services have a policy about. This was not good news. In the background, though, I heard a discussion about giving an individual a manicure and facial. I couldn't help feeling cheered that someone was offering good care.

. . . .

The standard of care you should be able to expect

If you, or a relative or friend is receiving care in a nursing or care home, you are entitled to care that is consistent with the following 'Person-Centred Values' and to raise concerns if these are not being delivered:

- Privacy – for example, the professional staff member should knock on the door and wait for a response before opening the door.

- Choice – individuals receiving the service should, for example, be able to choose what they want to eat, or wear, or the time they get up and go to bed, how to decorate their personal space etc.
- Respect – staff should treat everyone as they would like to be treated themselves.
- Dignity – individuals should be able to choose who they would like to support them with their personal care. The individual's background or culture might demand, for example, that it has to be someone of the same sex as them.
- Independence – staff should enable and support individuals to do as much as they can for themselves, even if it is more efficient to do things for them.
- Individuality and identity – this means enabling individuals to express their personal tastes and preferences, such as dressing the way they want to, or decorating their bedrooms in the way they want.
- Rights – everyone has the right to education and freedom of thought, conscience and religion, freedom of expression, freedom of assembly and freedom from discrimination. Also not to be subjected to torture, inhuman or degrading treatment, to be given a fair trial, and the right to respect for private and family life, home and correspondence.
- Partnership – staff should work in partnership with the individuals they support to get the individuals' needs met.

Chapter 2

Mum is admitted to hospital with fractures

I awoke after a largely sleepless night, and found I couldn't finish my breakfast. I was just about to sit down in my study when the room began spinning. I was falling; I knew I was falling, but nothing was telling my brain to stop it. Something did, at least, tell me to curl up in the fetal position as my body knocked against the filing cabinet, bounced against the bookcase and hit the floor.

When I came to I didn't think I had been out for long and crawled along the floor into my bedroom. I knew I had fainted and guessed it was probably due to stress – the stress of knowing about poor practice in some of the services I was working with, mixed with my worry about my mother being hurt in her own nursing home. It took a few days in bed, mostly sleeping, before I got back my strength and the confidence to get up without feeling wobbly or passing out.

On 20 March, I got out of bed and turned my mobile on. A voicemail from the manager of my mother's nursing home told me that Mum's other leg had 'spontaneously broken'.

When I rang the manager she repeated that Mum's other leg had broken; there had been no accident; it just broke spontaneously because my mother was old. Mum was in hospital. Could this be true, I asked myself. Can bones just break like that? If bones are no longer load-bearing, I knew that osteoporosis was a risk, but... Could this new break be from the first accident with the hoist and just not been noticed, or reported, before? Or could there have been a new accident?

I rang the hospital to ask how Mum was. The staff nurse replied, 'She has a broken ankle on one leg and a fractured femur on the other leg.'

'Thank you for confirming that,' I said. 'Are you going to make this a Safeguarding issue?'

'Why?' asked the staff nurse.

'My mother is an older person who lives in a nursing home and has come into your hospital with not one, but two fractures. Don't you think that's a bit strange? It should be classed as a Safeguarding issue and investigated, surely?' The nurse agreed and said she would look into it.

I was not well enough to travel across London and down to the west coast by train to see Mum. Fortunately, my sister, Ann, was able to take us in the car and, although I didn't feel right, I needed to see Mum and find out what had happened.

I had caught the train down many times and usually stayed a few days. I enjoyed taking Mum out in a taxi to a café. The last time Mum and I had been to that café was with my brother, Keith, and we had had a cup of tea and chips. Keith had pushed Mum's wheelchair and Mum had enjoyed the fresh air. We had had photos taken, first of Mum and me and then of me and Keith. That had been a good day. We had taken Mum back to the home and I had returned to the east coast, my brother to his home. The seven-hour train journey hadn't seemed so bad as the beautiful day had kept going around in my head.

I asked my Aunty Ann if she would like to come with us as she usually did when we were going down by car to see Mum. We'd had good times going down all together. The last time the three of us had been to see Mum we had gone into the town and done some shopping: Mum, Aunty Ann, my sister Ann and me. Four sisters, I had said, as we sat munching cake in a restaurant, mentally photographing the moment. When we went to see Mum it also gave my sister and me time together. We didn't live far from each other, but with busy lives we didn't often meet up. After buying things for Mum and her bedroom, we had headed towards the taxi rank where we had arranged for a black cab (as we had a wheelchair) to pick us up. It was only a little way up the road, but pushing a wheelchair was hard work and there were some really steep hills. Back at the nursing home, we had settled Mum with her magazines and taken the other purchases to her room. When we'd got back down to the lounge we saw Mum and Aunty Ann sitting together, chatting and reading magazines. I had quickly taken a photograph. We'd laughed and joked, despite knowing that before long the three of us would have to leave Mum and drive back home. It had not been easy, but we'd kept our emotions under control and left, knowing that we'd be down again the following month.

Now that we were driving down again, Aunty Ann was unable to come down to the hospital with us as she was not feeling up to it.

'If there is anything wrong, our Suey, I expect you to sort it out,' she told me as she gave me the chocolate she had bought for Mum. I knew they were all relying on me because of my work.

So four days after I'd had the first message about the 'spontaneous' second broken leg, my sister and I drove to the hospital. We stopped at the same service station as we always did – but it was different without Aunty Ann there.

'Accidents happen,' my sister said again. Did she want to believe that? I didn't answer her as I knew we would need to discuss it in detail later.

As we walked through the large entrance of the service station, my heart was heavy. I missed Aunty Ann being with us and was worried about her feeling unwell. I looked at the carpet and wanted to stamp my feet and scream like a child, 'I can't do this!' knowing how they were all expecting me to put things right. I took a deep breath and followed my sister to the toilets and then to get a cup of tea. Perhaps she was feeling the same because we both sat at the table quietly, not saying anything, and not doing anything until Ann said, 'Ready?' Then like robots we got up and walked out, across the car park to the car.

We didn't talk much as we drove. We dropped our stuff off at our usual B&B and drove to the hospital. Leaving the car in the hospital car park, we passed a pond with two mallard ducks waddling around it. We followed the signs for the wards and pressed the container on the wall to dispense some alcohol gel onto our hands before walking through the door. We looked around, and saw lots of different bays with beds in them and staff rushing about, before we explained to a staff nurse that we had come to see our mother.

'Have you found out how her injuries occurred?' I asked.

'No, not yet,' the nurse replied. 'But I do remember us speaking on the telephone a few days ago.'

I wanted to shake her; it was four days since she had said she would contact the home and find out.

'Don't you think it's strange that an older person from a nursing home comes in with a fractured ankle on one side and a fractured femur on the other side?' I asked her.

'Yes, it is. I'll ring through this evening.'

'I would have thought someone would have raised this as a Safeguarding issue by now. Can you do it whilst we're here, please?' I asked.

'Yes, of course.'

'We'll stay here whilst you do the call. *Now*,' I demanded, with as much steel as I could muster.

The staff nurse made the call and told us what the nurse at the home was saying as she spoke. The nurse at the home said that as Mum was being hoisted she fell through the hoist, landing on the floor with one leg beneath her. I felt ill. So much for spontaneous fractures!

We were directed to where Mum was. Before we reached her bed, my sister asked, 'What is "Safeguarding"?'

'In the profession we have a duty of care to keep vulnerable people safe,' I told her. 'Vulnerable people are people like Mum who are dependent on care in a home, or a hospital or in their own home. We, as paid professionals, have a responsibility to keep people safe and protect them from poor practices, harm, neglect or abuse.'

'Oh,' she replied.

'Older people and people with disabilities are likely to need Safeguarding,' I added.

Mum was propped up in bed and happy to see us. All my worry drained from me as I saw she was okay in herself. I told myself I shouldn't have worried so much. I had dreaded the worst, but I should have remembered that Mum had a high pain threshold. If I stubbed a toe, I would dance around complaining whereas Mum would say 'ouch' and get on with whatever she was doing.

My sister gave Mum the chocolates that Aunty Ann had asked us to take down.

'Can I have some now?' Mum wanted to know and I wondered why she would ask this.

We tried to talk about what had happened and Mum said, 'I'm not going back there.' When we asked why she just said, 'Can't say.' We tried to prompt her and she said that the staff shouted at her. We asked how the accident had happened and Mum clearly did not want to say. I wondered if it was fright from the accident, or fear of reprisals if she told someone what had happened. This made Ann and me feel useless, but we didn't pressurise Mum that evening. And there were more immediate things to concern us.

I noted that the contents of Mum's catheter bag were deep brown in colour. It didn't take specialist knowledge to understand that Mum must be dehydrated.

With one leg in plastic and the other ankle in plaster it was difficult for Mum to turn on her side. She could not reach her drink and we needed to help her. We told the nurses that she could not move and asked them to keep an eye on her and give her fluids. We also told the nurse of the colour of her urine in the catheter bag.

Ann and I went for something to eat. We discussed the visit and tried to work out what Mum was not telling us, but hadn't come to a conclusion before we went back to the B&B.

The following morning I rang Mum's nursing home to speak to the Manager and ask if my sister and I could visit to discuss how Mum had had her accident. The Manager was off duty, but the nurse said we could come. We agreed it would be later that morning as any earlier could interfere with the running of the home. My sister and I decided that I would do the talking.

So, after we had spent a short time with Mum at the hospital, we drove to the nursing home. My stomach flipped as we drew up. Ann rang the bell and we were let in. To our surprise, the Associate Director of the company that co-owned the nursing home was there, and he, the nurse we had spoken to on the telephone, Ann and I went into the office and discussed what had happened. Half-way through the meeting the Manager arrived.

The Associate Director said that Mum 'was slipping in the hoist and staff lowered her to the floor'.

I asked, 'Why was Mum slipping?'

'Staff had not crossed the hoist at the back. I hold my hands up; it is our fault,' he said, raising his arms in the air.

'The hospital said that Mum had been dropped and landed on her leg.'

He said, 'That did not happen.'

'He's lying,' I thought to myself.

'When are you going to investigate what happened?' I asked.

'I've already done an investigation. It's now complete. All staff will receive more frequent training on moving and handling. I'm the trainer.'

'I don't think your investigation can be complete as there's a discrepancy in reports of what happened,' I told him.

'The investigation is complete,' he repeated, but would not give me eye contact.

'Has this been raised in staff supervision sessions?' I asked.

He looked quite shocked when I mentioned the word 'supervision', and answered by saying, 'Staff will receive more training on moving and handling.'

'Yes, but has it been discussed in their supervision session so they can reflect on what happened? And something needs to be written in their files.'

'They've been told that they should have called the ambulance straight away.'

'W-hat?'

'They did not follow company policy and call the ambulance straight away. The Manager did it when she came into work – the following morning,' he told us.

I was appalled – and furious!

'When your mother comes back we'll ensure nothing like this happens again,' the Associate Director assured us.

'You should have ensured that before,' I told him. 'Besides, Mum said last night that she doesn't want to come back here.'

When he promised they would take care of her, I had to try to stop my facial expression saying what I was thinking. There was silence in the room and I knew it was time to leave.

In the car, Ann and I dissected the meeting and were both very angry. We both independently had thought we were not being told the whole story.

We called into a supermarket to get some food and fill the car up with petrol; then spent a few hours with Mum in hospital before heading home to the east coast. We got stuck on the M25 and to make sure this didn't feed our anger we tried to do a crossword; we were both hopeless and it made us laugh… just what we needed.

. . . .

What you need to know if you are in this situation

Staff working in the Social Care and Health sectors have a duty of care:

- This means that they have a paid duty to keep vulnerable people safe, and
- A responsibility to protect them from any poor practices, harm, neglect or abuse.

Vulnerable people are those over the age of 18 who are unable to take care of themselves and/or unable to protect themselves from harm and abuse.

If you receive poor care:

- Contact a relative or friend and tell them what has happened if you're not confident about addressing the problem by yourself.
- Ask them to go with you to the manager to discuss what happened with you.
- Keep a diary of the incident and all meetings and discussions.
- If you feel comfortable, ask for a copy of the organisation's complaints procedure or you may be able to get it from the internet, if you have access to the internet. Alternatively, you can follow the complaints procedure as described in the appendix at the back of this book.

If you are concerned about the care a relative, friend, or someone you know is receiving:

- Get the facts.
- Ask for a meeting with the manager of the care/nursing home.
- Ask what they will put in place so it doesn't happen again.
- Ask the individual who has been affected what s/he wants to happen. (it may be best to ask them away from the manager/staff so they can give an objective view and not feel that they have to say what they feel the manager/staff would want them to say).
- Ask for a copy of the complaints procedure or you may be able to access it from the internet. Alternatively, you can follow the complaints procedure described in the appendix at the back of this book.

Chapter 3

Pressure

I was very concerned about Mum's injuries and the fact that I could not get a clear account of what had happened to her. Her refusal to talk about it added to my worry. I realised I had to take things to a higher level and make a complaint to the organisation responsible for Safeguarding vulnerable people – like my mother – in care and nursing homes.

When Mum had her accident in March 2009, the regulation of social care in England was carried out by a government body called the Commission for Social Care Inspection, or CSCI, and the regulation of health services was carried out by the Healthcare Commission, or HC. However, almost immediately (1 April) both of these bodies were replaced by the new Care Quality Commission, or CQC. This was to cause me a lot of difficulty as this meant a brand new organisation that was finding its feet was now responsible for auditing my mother's nursing home.

The remit of the CQC (www.cqc.org.uk) was – and is – the independent regulation of health and social care in England, including in hospitals, dental practices, ambulances, care homes, people's own homes and elsewhere. It is responsible for registering services if they meet government standards, can make unannounced inspections of services – both planned visits and in response to concerns – and carries out investigations into why care fails to improve. It monitors the information that it collects and has a range of powers to take action if people are getting poor care. The manager of a home is obliged to notify the CQC of accidents and incidents and the CQC must then inform the local Safeguarding Team for that area.

Each area across England has a Safeguarding Team and the focus of Safeguarding is prevention and protection of vulnerable adults and children. It has an alerting role when Safeguarding concerns or potential risks arise. This involves sharing information with agencies such as police and Social Services. Their ultimate responsibility is to the adult or child in need or at risk.

I looked for the telephone number of the Care Quality Commission, pressed the call button and heard it ring through to the Newcastle office. They asked what area my mother lived in and, when I told them, put me through to Sarah, CQC Inspector for the area in which the nursing home was situated.

After discussing my concerns, Sarah said that she was happy with what the home had put in place. I told her I wasn't happy and that I was also concerned about Mum's care in the hospital (of which I will say more very shortly) and that I had been trying to get hold of the Safeguarding Lead Manager for the area but, although I had left numerous messages, he had not returned my calls. Sarah rang him that same day, then rang me back to say that she had discussed my concerns with him and he would call me later.

About a week later, he did finally ring. He said that Mum was vulnerable in the hospital and should have a social worker allocated to her; he would arrange one for her. He added that he would ask Isabel, Team Leader of the Safeguarding Unit, to ring me.

I rang the Safeguarding Lead Manager several times over the weeks that followed to say that I was still waiting to hear from Isabel. He apologised and said he would make sure that she rang me. When she did eventually call me she repeated what I had heard from Sarah – that the Care Quality Commission were happy with what the home had put in place.

'What are they going to put in place?' I asked her.

'The home said that they didn't respond as they should have done; the third member of staff could not attend as your mother was on the third floor.'

'Why couldn't the third member of staff get up to Mum's floor?' I asked.

'I don't know,' she replied.

Whilst discussing Mum's fracture, it became clear that Isabel was unaware that Mum had two fractures.

'I didn't know there was a second injury. I will ask the nursing home for more information,' Isabel said.

I then raised a new concern that I had only become aware of more recently.

'I would also like to complain about Mum having a grade 2 pressure sore while she was in the nursing home,' I told her.

'How do you know she had it when she was in the nursing home?' she asked me.

'Because the hospital nursing staff told me about it this morning when I rang to ask how Mum was. They said she had had the sore when she was admitted.'

'Let me finish finding out how the accident happened. Then you can start this further enquiry.' She told me this would involve me making a separate complaint and her following it up, again separately. I found this hard to believe. I argued that both cases should be investigated together, but she would not agree.

I also told Isabel that I had contacted the Health and Safety Executive to ask if Mum's accident had been reported under the 'Reporting of Injuries, Diseases and Dangerous Occurrences Regulations' (otherwise known as 'RIDDOR') and had been told it had not. She did not give a response to this. (If a resident has an accident in a care home the manager of the home should report it under the Health and Safety Act 1974.) The call ended.

*

I was indeed concerned about Mum's care in the hospital. When she had been admitted she had, apparently, had a 'grade 2 pressure sore', though I had only just been told about this. It had since got worse and was now a 'grade 4' – the worst possible. I had, of course, heard of pressure sores, or 'bed sores', but knowing little I did some research on the internet. I found the following:

> *Pressure sores (also known as bedsores or decubitus ulcers) are ulcers of the skin (due to pressure) causing a lack of blood supply to the area. Pressure sores are categorised into 4 stages of severity:*
> *Grade 1 – reddened skin which persists for more than 30 minutes after pressure has been relieved.*
> *Grade 2 – superficial skin damage. May present as a blister or as an abrasion.*
> *Grade 3 – full thickness skin loss not extending to bone or muscle. This grade is not usually painful.*
> *Grade 4 – full thickness skin loss with extensive tissue damage through muscle and bone.*
> *www.judy-waterlow.co.uk/pressure-sore-symptoms.htm*

I looked at photos of the different grades; when I got to grade 4 I rushed to the bathroom and vomited. Then I sat on the floor and cried. I could not believe it. By now my mother had this terrible injury that would take months, or even longer, to heal.

Given the hospital had let things get this bad, how could I trust them to put things right? She had been in their care for five weeks before they even bothered to tell us about the pressure sores, and then they had just dropped it into the conversation as if it were an everyday occurrence. Perhaps it was for them? The treatment they had now prescribed – for the pressure sores – consisted of a specialist nurse (called the 'tissue viability nurse') cleaning the ulcerated area regularly and applying dressings, while a programme had been set up to turn Mum regularly to relieve pressure so long as she was immobile. I could not trust them to follow through on this plan. I did not even know if this was the best treatment they could offer. I just did not know how to help Mum get better.

I contacted the Safeguarding Lead Manager again and told him of my concerns about the care the hospital was providing. He said that he would ask the Director of Nursing to ring me to discuss these. I added that I was sure Mum was vulnerable on the ward. He reiterated that she should have a social worker to look after her interests whilst she was in hospital and he would arrange for this to happen.

. . . .

What you need to know about pressure sores

Anybody who is bedbound, or a wheelchair user, is at risk of developing pressure sores. Issues with incontinence increase the risk as wet skin is more vulnerable. It is important to be aware that the sufferer may not feel pain or be aware that anything is wrong until the sore has gone very deep, by which stage it will be extremely difficult to heal.

There are two further very important things to be aware of. The first is that pressure sores can kill. They may become an open wound that can lead to blood poisoning – 'septicaemia' – if they become infected and the infection is not properly treated.

The second is that, while a person may be at risk, good nursing – such as turning a bedbound patient frequently (see below) – will prevent her/him developing sores in the first place. Pressure sores are a sign of neglect.

Pressure ulcers are a painful, debilitating and potentially serious outcome of a failure to provide sufficient nursing or medical care. Reference: Bennett G, Dealey C, Posnett J (2004) The cost of pressure ulcers in the UK. Age Ageing 33(3): 230–5

A nurse or doctor could be negligent if a patient is harmed because of ignorance of well-accepted and well-known published nursing and medical research findings.
Reference: Tingle J (2002) Clinical negligence and the need to keep professionally updated. British Journal of Nursing 11(20): 1304–6

To expand on the information on Judy Waterlow's website, there are four recognised grades of pressure ulcers in the EPUAP (European Pressure Ulcer Advisory Panel) Wound Classification system.

- Grade 1: The skin is intact but discoloured and the discolouration is not affected by light finger pressure ('non-blanching erythema'), nor does it disappear after pressure has been relieved for 30 minutes. This can be difficult to identify in darkly pigmented skin.
- Grade 2: Partial-thickness skin loss or damage involving the 'epidermis' (outer layer of skin). The grade 2 pressure ulcer is superficial and looks like a graze, blister or shallow crater.
- Grade 3: Full thickness skin loss involving damage to subcutaneous tissue (that is, tissue below the full thickness of the skin) but not extending to the muscles and bone. The grade 3 pressure ulcer looks like a deep crater and the neighbouring tissue may also be undermined.
- Grade 4: Full thickness skin loss with extensive destruction and 'necrosis' extending to the underlying muscle and bone. 'Necrosis' means that there is actual cell death – that part of the body affected is starting to die!

With higher stages of ulcer, healing time is prolonged. While about 75% of grade 2 ulcers heal within eight weeks, only 62% of grade 4 pressure ulcers ever heal, and only 52% heal within one year. (Reference: Thomas DR, Diebold MR, Eggemeyer LM (2005).

A controlled, randomized, comparative study of a radiant heat bandage on the healing of stage 3–4 pressure ulcers: a pilot study. *Journal of the American Medical Directors Association*, 6 (1): 46-49.) Infection delays healing of minor sores and can be life threatening in deeper sores. It can even enter the bone, requiring weeks of treatment with antibiotics. In the most severe cases, infection can spread into the bloodstream. Signs of infection include an unpleasant smell coming from the sore and warm or swollen skin around the area.

For most people, pressure sores cause some pain and itching. However, in people whose senses are dulled, even severe, deep sores may be painless.

For more information and photos of the 4 stages go to: http://www.judy-waterlow.co.uk/pressure-sore-symptoms.htm

For anybody who is bedbound or a wheelchair user or spends a lot of time in one position, staff should be:
- Reading the care plan and if it says to apply cream to the areas that are most at risk then they should do so
- Following a care plan that states how often the person should be turned/transferred
- Turning her/him in bed, or transferring her/him from the wheelchair to another seat.

Chapter 4

Going around in circles

The week after we were told about the pressure sores, I had a phone call from my brother to say he had visited Mum and she had been crying and holding onto the bed rails, she was in so much pain. Mum was one of those people who never complained, so we were both shocked things could have got this bad.

I rearranged some of my work and got the train down to see her the following day. I enjoyed the train trip, which brought back memories of my childhood, but was relieved when the journey was over. It was getting late. I bought some food in the supermarket and got a taxi to the usual B&B.

The next morning, I found Mum had been moved to a different bay. She was happy to see me and proudly told the patient in the next bed who I was. She looked happy, which was a great relief after what I had heard from my brother. However, she was having difficulty eating and drinking. She had tried different foods, including yogurts and sweet puddings, but still couldn't manage to eat them.

A staff nurse and I tried to ascertain from Mum what she would like to eat. She said, 'I don't want anything, thank you.'

'You need to eat, Mum,' I pleaded.

'Nothing, thank you.'

'What about some soft pears, or melon?' I asked.

'Or some grapes?' asked the nurse.

'I don't like grapes, but I could try some melon if you have some.'

I felt that there was a light at the end of the tunnel.

'We don't have melon,' the staff nurse told Mum. I waited for her to say that she would ask the cooks to get one or they would ring one of the nursing staff at home and ask her/him to bring one in on the late shift later, just as I had done when I managed residential services. She didn't.

'Oh, okay; I can get the bus into town and buy a melon,' I said, again waiting for the staff nurse to say that there was no need to do that. But she didn't, so I arranged for a nurse to look out for Mum whilst I was gone. I went out in the rain and waited at the bus stop. I could not believe that I had felt the need to ask a nurse to look after Mum. In a hospital, what else should they have been doing?

I caught the bus into town and bought two melons. Back at the hospital I used the alcohol gel and went back onto the ward. I gave the melons to a healthcare assistant and asked her to cut a piece for Mum when she woke up. I sat by Mum's bed whilst she slept. Later she ate a little of the evening meal followed by a small piece of melon.

'I'm sorry, I have tried to eat it,' she told me.

'I know you're trying, Mum. Please don't worry,' I replied.

The next three days were like *Groundhog Day*. The only difference between each was that on the third day of my visit I actually saw Mum hold onto the bed rail and cry with pain, as my brother had described. This seemed to be from the pressure sores, which were preventing her from moving. The nurses gave her paracetamol. I asked for stronger pain killers, but they didn't give her any.

Back at home, catching up with work and emails, I received a series of calls.

The first was from the Ward Sister – that is, the nurse in charge of the ward:

'I'm ringing to ask if your mum is going back to the nursing home?'

'I'm really shocked to hear you ask this. Not only because of what happened to Mum at the home. You know we're waiting for a social worker so she can be assessed for nursing care and I can go and look at a new nursing home for her?'

'Oh yes, of course you are.'

The Ward Sister updated me on Mum's pressure sore, and I asked, 'Are you going to raise this as a Safeguarding issue against the home?'

'Why?' she asked. I reiterated what I had told the staff nurse with whom I'd discussed the issue before: 'Mum is an older person coming in from a nursing home with two broken legs...'

'I don't know...,' she replied.

'Why don't you know when you're the Ward Sister?'

'I don't, but I'll get the Director of Nursing to telephone you.' And we finished the call.

The telephone call from the Director of Nursing was unsatisfactory:

'The hospital took out a Safeguarding issue on 3rd April against the nursing home on your mother being admitted with her broken legs and, in the week commencing 20th April, the nursing home took out a Safeguarding issue against the hospital because of the pressure sores.' He paused after delivering this only partially satisfactory news. Then he asked, 'How are you getting on with looking for a new home?'

'I've been told I can't do anything until a social worker is in place and can do an assessment,' I told him.

'Your mum has got a social worker to help her find a new home,' he replied.

'No, I'm sure she hasn't,' I said firmly. 'One of the staff nurses gave me a phone number for us to call and when my brother rang it he was told they had heard nothing about my mother.'

'Oh, I'll look into that.'

Later I telephoned the hospital:

'I'm ringing to ask how my mum is.'

'Oh, I'm just preparing for her discharge back to the nursing home,' said the discharge person.

'What?!' I was really shocked. 'She is not going back there,' I declared, and explained why. 'I've already had a long conversation with the Ward Sister stating all this,' I told her in a way that reflected my extreme irritation. I spelt out to her that my brother was the next of kin, so she would need to check any decisions out with him, but I could assure her that Mum was not going back to her previous home.

'Oh, I'd better check with my own team first and get my records up to date,' she responded.

'You better had,' I thought.

Later again that same day, I received a call from a director of the nursing home's parent company:

'Is your mother returning to the nursing home?'

There was something about this phone call that put me on edge, not least the timing. Was it coincidence that on the same day I had been talking about Safeguarding issues with the hospital, the nursing home's parent company decided to ring me? Perhaps it was me being suspicious, but I felt that the hospital and the nursing home company were going to bat things to and fro between them. Would I be caught in the middle as my mother's daughter?

'The family is totally shocked about everything at the moment. Your company is supposed to protect vulnerable people, but it didn't protect my mother, did it?' I asked, not really expecting an answer.

'I am sorry to trouble you at this time; we'll talk again when you're ready,' he said and we ended the call.

I rang my sister to talk through my suspicions. Like me, she thought something underhand was going on. But what could we do? We needed to focus on making sure Mum got good care and moved to a nursing home that would look after her properly.

. . . .

If you find yourself in this situation

Finding yourself pitted against one or more big institutions is exceedingly difficult, especially when the person you care about is essentially at the mercy of one of these. It is very important to write notes of each event, meeting and telephone discussion that takes place so that you can keep track of events and point to future inconsistencies in information and excuses that you are given.

At the same time, you must not lose sight of the most important goal – to ensure the person you care for is safe, happy and receiving good care. If this means putting accusations and recriminations to one side – temporarily – then you can promise yourself you will return to that battle later, when the time is right.

There is no one person that can help when you are pitted against an organisation; you will find you have to follow their individual complaints procedure.

- Speak to the Ward Sister or senior nurse.
- You can also talk to the Patient Advice and Liaison Service (PALS) – every hospital has a PALS office that you can walk into and share concerns with.
- Keep detailed notes of all meetings, telephone calls, conversations and events, and write these up (with the date) while the memory is still fresh.
- Never give up!

Chapter 5

Caring – the cracks grow wider

My brother called me late the next day.

'I went to see Mum this evening,' he told me.

'Oh good. How was she?' I asked, even though I had only left her the morning before.

'She's been holding onto the bed rails again, and crying,' he told me, and I wanted to cry.

'What did the nurse say when you told her?'

'I haven't told anyone, only you.'

'Why didn't you tell the nurse?' I asked.

Silence.

'Okay, I'll try and get down next week.'

Another train journey down to the hospital. The staff and I smiled at each other as I walked to Mum's bed. I could see she was in a lot of pain from her facial expression and the pinching of her eyebrows. I didn't think she heard or understood the staff nurse at the end of her bed asking if she wanted any painkillers, as she said she didn't. Within minutes, though, she was crying with pain and holding on to the bed rail, as my brother had described. I tried to comfort her.

'Can you give my mother some painkillers, please?' I pleaded.

'I can't unless the patient agrees to take them,' the staff nurse told me.

'I know you can't legally give tablets if a patient refuses them, but surely there is something else you can do. Perhaps test for capacity?' I suggested, hoping that she would do something. She didn't. She carried on fiddling with things in the drug trolley and did not reply to my question. I had suggested testing for capacity just in case Mum was having difficulty making decisions.

'Mum, if you had any pain where would it be?' I asked.

'In my chest and lower back,' she replied.

'There you are,' I said to the staff nurse. 'Can you now ask my mum if she would like some painkillers to take the pain away?' The nurse asked and Mum accepted.

On many occasions after this, I told doctors and qualified nurses that Mum was in pain and asked for something stronger to help her. It was excruciating watching a very proud woman cling to the bed rail and cry. After more than six weeks on this ward, Mum was still deprived of stronger pain relief; they only gave paracetamol. They would not tell me why and they would not give anything stronger. After a while the doctor started to say that he thought Mum was depressed.

Every time I was on the ward, I explained to the nurses and the doctor how to communicate with my mother, a proud woman who did not like to admit to weakness and also might sometimes not understand what was being asked of her. I told them, 'Ask, "Are you in any pain?" and Mum will say "No". Ask her, "If you had any pain where would it be?" and she'll then admit to being in pain and where, usually in the lower back and in her chest.' Although I took time to explain this to each staff nurse, most clearly did not wish even to acknowledge that I was talking, let alone what I was saying, and it appeared that they were going to ignore me, even when they were at the end of her bed with the drug trolley. An assessment of pain should include an assessment of body language and non-verbal cues (such as loss of appetite, or grimacing) (see www.epuap.org/guidelines/Final_Quick_Treatment.pdf).

Mum was on a 'turning programme' for her pressure sores. This involves a patient being regularly moved to a new position to prevent pressure on the problem areas and to prevent new sores forming. However, I noticed when I was with her she was not always turned two-hourly as the doctor had stipulated. I reported this first to the nurses and then finally to the doctor, hoping he could tell the nurses it needed to be done. I also explained to him about the way the nurses should ask Mum if she was in pain; he said I should tell them, they wouldn't mind. I told him that I continually told the staff and they were still not doing what was needed. He agreed to have a word with them, but nothing seemed to change. Whenever I returned to the ward Mum would have slid down, or be leaning over the left side of the bed.

The day after my conversation with the doctor, I entered the ward and, as I walked towards Mum's bed, I could see she was slumped over the side of it. Not again! I asked two nurses, who had finished hoisting the patient in the next bed, to sit my mother upright. To my relief they agreed and arranged to wash her at the same time. I did my usual sitting outside the ward whilst they pulled the curtains around the bed, hoisted Mum, washed her and made her comfortable. I felt pleased this was being done, but also shocked that I should have to remind the staff to do what was only their job.

I called the hospital the next day.

'Hi, how's my mum?'

'She's not eating or drinking well.'

'Can she be put on a drip?' I asked.

'We wouldn't do that because your mum would become dependent on it, and we don't want that,' said the staff nurse.

'If Mum isn't drinking, then she could become dehydrated. She can't move because of the pressure sore. Do you want her to die?' I asked her.

'No, we don't want that,' the staff nurse replied matter of factly, with no compassion in her voice.

I explained how to ascertain if Mum was in pain and the staff nurse reluctantly said, 'I'll try it on my shift, but I can't guarantee that the other staff will do it when I'm not on.'

'Can it be recorded on Mum's notes, for consistency?' I asked.

'No, it can't, as more important information's recorded and passed on during hand over.'

I called the hospital again the following morning.

'I'm ringing to ask how my mum is.'

'She's okay.'

'What does okay mean?'

'I don't know. I'm the ward clerk; I'll go and ask a nurse.'

A staff nurse came on the phone and introduced herself.

'How is my mum today?' I asked.

'She's alright.'

'What does "alright" mean?'

'Well, she took her tablets, but she hasn't had anything to eat.'

'Well, then she's not okay, is she?'

The next time I was on the ward, I told the Ward Sister who was on duty that I was looking forward to the Safeguarding meeting, scheduled for the following day. To my dismay (though I should not have been surprised by this stage) she did not appear to know that this had been planned with her and the Director of Nursing. I explained that the Director of Nursing and I had had a telephone conversation and arranged a date to hold the meeting, which was now tomorrow. I had assumed she would have received an email, but, I asked myself, when does a Ward Sister have time to look at emails?

The Ward Sister said she had never taken part in a Safeguarding meeting before, so I briefly explained what they were like, wondering what this situation would be like for the relative of a patient who was not familiar with 'the system'. I told her of my concerns about lack of communication, and incorrect communication with her staff.

'We've had complaints before about communication. I don't know what to do about it,' she confessed.

'Have you thought of using the Named Nurse system?' I asked. 'That way, one of my family could ring in to one specific nurse and receive consistent reports back.'

'I like that idea,' she acknowledged. 'It would help to stop the complaints about communication. I'll see if it can be rolled out across the ward for all patients.'

I sat outside of the ward and sent a text to my sister to ask her to bring nail varnish and manicure stuff to do Mum's nails; then I went outdoors. I tried to read the paper but I found 'people watching' easier. It was hard to concentrate on reading, knowing that I had a full day ahead of me, observing the staff, making sure they did their jobs properly. I also had my work on my mind. As a consultant who worked alone, it was very hard to take all this time away and not adversely affect my business

When I returned to the ward, Mum was on her side in the bed looking out of the window. She was happy to see me.

'Hi, Mum, how are you?' I asked.

'Can't grumble', replied my mother. I smiled. I wished she would grumble to the nurses now and again. Because we had spent so much time together, we had very little to say to each other, but I felt it was important that I was there to 'watch her back'. Mum drifted off to sleep throughout the morning and it gave me a chance to try and read the newspaper as well as keeping an eye on things on the ward.

I was so tired. My mother had been in hospital for seven weeks now. I was constantly shattered from travelling down to the hospital from the east coast as often as work would allow and then being around the bed or on the ward watching out for Mum. I often wondered if I was invading her privacy or making her uncomfortable by being there so much. If I was in a hospital bed I don't think I would like someone there nearly 24/7, looking at me, making small talk and just constantly being there.

In a break outside, I chatted to another visitor who had come to see her husband. She got emotional as she told me she was losing him and didn't know what to do. She asked who I was visiting; I told her it was my mother. I did not tell her anything about the standard of care, not wanting to cry to a stranger – I was exhausted and very emotional. I tried to comfort and listen to her. Mainly she recalled happy events and acknowledged that her husband had had a 'good innings' – he was 92 years old, she told me. I smiled and we stood up and hugged; then she walked back into the hospital. I walked along the path and swallowed back the tears before going back in myself.

Back on the ward Mum was asking for some water; I poured her some from the jug and she drank it. We knew it was tea time as the smell of food filled the ward. She couldn't remember what she had ordered earlier, but I tried to keep her positive about eating.

I waited for the staff to finish with the patient they were helping before I asked them to turn Mum. They pulled the curtains round Mum's bed and hoisted her whilst I stared out of the window, watching people come and go.

I thanked the nurses and then applied alcohol gel to mine and Mum's hands. We made a joke about the horrible smell, but both agreed it would keep us free from germs, even though the ward was lovely and clean. No complaints there.

'Can I help you with your tea, Mum?'

'Course you can, love, if you want to.'

I did want to feed her because Mum had to stay on her side – a very difficult position to eat in – but I did my best to give her respect and dignity by asking her.

I was feeding Mum at a steady pace and asking her if she wanted a sip of her drink after each mouthful. It was a slow process as she didn't really want to eat any more, but she was losing weight and needed to counteract that. To my disbelief, while we were doing this an impatient healthcare assistant (the role that used to be known as an 'auxiliary nurse') pushed me out of the way and took the spoon from my hand. She shovelled the food into Mum's mouth so quickly that I didn't have time to say anything. When she had finished she dropped the spoon onto the bed table and left. Mum was retching and I had to rub her back and comfort and reassure her.

I had not met this healthcare assistant before, nor the female staff nurse who was administering medication. I was surprised when this nurse seemed quite agitated that I was there. She was the only one to tell me, in an aggressive way, to get off the ward as it was restricted at meal times. I had never considered before why I was the only visitor on the ward during meal times. I explained that I had been allowed to stay, and that I was glad that I had or my mum would have been retching more often after being force-fed with no one to help her.

When the healthcare assistant returned, I asked her to come to one side and explained what she had done. I was *so* angry! She said that they only had a limited period of time to do meals and that she loved my mother and that she was sorry. She left the area and carried on with her work. I comforted Mum, and when it was time for her two-hourly turn I told her I was leaving and that my sister would be with her in the next few hours. As the two nurses approached Mum and began talking to her, I said cheerio and let them know that my sister would be along in an hour.

It had been a long, emotional day and I was glad to be leaving the hospital. I stopped as usual to look at the ducks and to gather my thoughts. I decided to walk back to the B&B to try to clear my head. I wondered if Mum had been force-fed before when I hadn't been there. The thought made me shudder.

Back at the B&B, I received a call from the Director of Nursing to confirm I would be at the meeting the following day. I explained my sister was coming to see Mum and would also be attending the meeting. It was during this conversation that I expressed concern at what the healthcare assistant had done.

'You should talk to the Ward Sister about any concerns you have,' was the Director of Nursing's reply.

'The Safeguarding Adults Manager told me to liaise with you about any concerns I have,' I replied. 'This happened today so I was going to bring it up tomorrow, but I'm just mentioning it now.'

The Director of Nursing blustered, 'Oh well, of course you can tell me. Of course you can.'

Ann met me outside the B&B. I asked her if she would mind going in to see Mum by herself that evening so I could have a bit of a break. We arranged a time to meet for supper and I waved my sister off as she drove to the hospital. It was horrible to admit that I was glad of a free evening, away from monitoring the nurses all the time.

At supper, my sister told me how pleased Mum had been to see her and that she liked having had her nails filed and polished.

We talked about tomorrow's meeting and ensured I had all our concerns written down. We discussed what needed to be done for Mum, and how we could all do our fair share. I suggested that I should be responsible for looking into Safeguarding issues and looking for a new home; Ann could be responsible for ringing in to the designated nurse for updates when I was not at the hospital; and our brother could continue to visit when possible. She agreed. I also asked her to tell Keith, even though I felt as though I was passing the buck.

· ·

If you are worried about the care your loved one is getting in hospital:

- Ask for a meeting to discuss the care. This meeting should be with the Ward Sister/charge nurse of the ward in the first instance.

- Follow the hospital's complaint procedure.
- Ring or visit the Patient Advice and Liaison Services (PALS) office, which will be situated in the hospital.
- Action on Elder Abuse UK Helpline: 080 8808 8141 (The number will not appear on your telephone bill.) www. elderabuse.org.uk
- Contact your local Age UK shop / office.
- Contact your local Healthwatch office.
- Report your concerns to the Care Quality Commission.

Chapter 6

Meeting with the Director of Nursing and the Ward Sister

My sister and I spent some time with Mum before going into the meeting with the Ward Sister and the Director of Nursing. When the meeting began, the Director of Nursing said he would write the minutes and we would receive a copy. (We never did.) We sat in a small room which was not big enough for four to meet comfortably, but we were grateful for the meeting so things could, we hoped, be put right.

The first thing on our list was that whenever we rang in to find out how our mother was, we had to talk to a variety of people and still did not get the information we wanted. We said we wanted a 'Named Nurse', so when Ann rang in she could speak to that nurse every time, and that nurse would be able to give her up-to-date and *correct* information. The Ward Sister had, of course, known that we would raise this, so she was ready to give us the name of our Named Nurse. She asked Ann to make contact with this person as soon as she could.

Our next concern was also about communication. The hospital had forms to be completed for each patient on how a patient communicates, but these did not give space to include how a patient communicates non-verbally. We discussed what needed to be on the form and I showed them an example in my *Effective Communication* workbook that was soon to be published. They liked the ideas in the workbook and said they would use extracts from it.

We then had a more specific issue. The secretary of the Consultant with overall responsibility for Mum's care had told our niece (my brother Keith's daughter) that there was to be a case conference today to discuss Mum going back to the nursing home. We needed to reiterate that Mum was *not* going back there. 'I wasn't aware of the meeting,' said the Ward Sister as she wrote something down. There was no embarrassment about this repeated failure to grasp the situation and the concerns we had about the nursing home.

I told the meeting about how we had decided to share responsibilities within the family. Neither the Ward Sister nor the Director of Nursing batted an eyelid when I said, 'I will be responsible for following up Safeguarding issues.'

'Mum doesn't always complain of pain, as she doesn't want to be a burden,' I said, 'but at times it's severe and she'll cry out and hold onto the bed rail. The pain is clearly intense and she can't move herself away from it because she's immobile.' The Ward Sister looked to the Director of Nursing, who was writing. 'Mum has said that she's had pain in her chest, her catheter and mostly her back.' I told them. I added that on some occasions, when I had explained to the nurse that Mum was in pain, the nurse had come and given her a cuddle, regardless of whether my mother wanted that contact or not. The Ward Sister looked to the Director of Nursing, again, who was still writing.

'I was really shocked to hear that my mother had lost one and a half stone within three weeks. How far will you let this weight loss go before you do something?' Ann asked the Ward Sister.

'It won't come to that. I wouldn't let it go too far,' replied the Ward Sister, but did not say what she would do to prevent it getting that far, nor what 'too far' actually might be.

I asked about my many previous requests for my mother to go onto nutritional drinks and the fact that this had not happened. We were assured that the dietician would be called to arrange for Mum to be written up for the nutritional drink, 'Ensure'. There was no explanation as to why this had not happened before.

As Mum was not eating or drinking much, I asked for her to have more water with her medication and a straw in a beaker – as opposed to an undignified and childlike teat.

'Good ideas,' agreed the Ward Sister. 'Bloody common sense, actually,' I thought to myself.

'How often is the catheter checked?' I asked. 'My mother may be able to fiddle with it and this could be a cause of the pain she's suffering.' Then, for good measure, 'And how often does she have a bladder wash?'

'It's almost impossible to pull the catheter out and it would or should be checked when your mother is turned,' the Ward Sister replied. 'I'm unable to say if your mother has had a bladder wash.'

'Why has Mum got the worst pressure sore – a grade 4?' I asked. I did not get a direct answer to that question.

'I'm looking into why the hospital has a high pressure sore rate and will let you know the outcome,' the Director of Nursing told us. It was not reassuring to know the rate was high.

'Mum is not always turned two-hourly and at times she's turned and put on her back.'

'Your mother can go up to four hours without being turned,' said the Ward Sister.

'So why is it that her notes say she must be turned every two hours?' I did not get an answer and looked over to the Director of Nursing, who was still writing.

I then told the meeting about the healthcare assistant who had shovelled food into Mum's mouth the night before and made her retch. We were told that the Ward Sister woud look into what had happened.

At the end of the meeting I expressed concern about having to leave Mum in the hospital when I needed to get back to the east coast that night. I was assured that everything would be done to look after Mum.

'I felt he was paying us lip service,' I said to Ann as we drove home.

'I agree,' she replied.

We agreed that it would be a good idea for us to record everything. I had already started making notes of things I was not happy with and suggested Ann made notes of her phone calls to the hospital. Just in case we needed evidence that things were not right.

Later that evening I had a call from an NVQ candidate called Jan.

'Hi Jan, how are you?'

'I've got a problem, Suzan, and need some advice,' Jan told me. Her tone told me something was really wrong.

'Okay, but as you know, it depends on what you tell me as to what I do with the information.'

'I'm really enjoying going into people's home but I've got some problems.' I purposely didn't say anything and waited for her to continue.

'I am caring for an elderly lady and I saw her husband take money out of her purse. He told me not to say anything.'

'So have you done anything about it as yet?'

'I reported it to Social Services. They investigated, but the lady doesn't want to get her husband into trouble. So nothing is going to be done.'

All I could do was sympathise with Jan's concern and make a mental note that Jan was a responsible and supportive worker. It is not in my remit to advise on something like this; once it has been reported as a Safeguarding issue to Social Services for them to investigate and advise on.

. . . .

If you need to hold a meeting with a hospital to discuss concerns:
- Discuss the issues with the Ward Sister first.
- Take your action as high up the organisation as possible.

- Prepare – write a list of all the things you are unhappy with, and
- Work out what you want from the meeting.
- If there is more than one of you decide who is going to be the speaker and who will take notes.
- At the meeting tell the representatives of the hospital the things you are happy with before telling them the things that are wrong.
- Take notes of everything that is said to compare with notes the hospital takes (if it does this) and send copies to all the people who attended if the hospital does not do this.
- Ensure the hospital formulates an action point with dates for follow-up, to check things have improved. Remind them about this if necessary.

Chapter 7

Sudden loss

My sister rang me to tell me some bad and unexpected news. Our aunt – my mother's sister and a big part of mine and my sister's lives – had suddenly been taken ill and was now in hospital. I remembered how she had not felt well enough to come with us in the car three weeks before, but I had never guessed she might need hospital care. This meant our mother and our aunt were now both in hospital, but many miles apart, with Mum on the west coast and Aunty Ann on the east coast.

I rang the east coast hospital and asked how my aunt was. They wouldn't give any information over the phone unless I was the next of kin. I appreciated the confidentiality, but I was desperate to know. I texted my cousins but didn't get any answers. Obviously they would not have their phones on in the hospital, I told myself.

I got in the car and drove to the hospital. I arrived just as my sister was coming out. We hugged. Did we have to keep meeting like this?

I went up to the ward and met my cousins who were sitting around Aunty Ann's bed. Aunty Ann was on diamorphine (that is a very strong pain killer) and very poorly. She wanted to be moved in the bed and needed hoisting. One of my cousins went and told a nurse. It was quite some time later when two nurses come and repositioned Aunty Ann in her bed. We waited at the top of the ward whilst this was being done.

As the nurses pulled back the curtains around the bed I asked my cousins, 'Can I go in and see Aunty Ann by myself?' They nodded. We were all one step away from the flood gates opening but we tried to keep them closed. I approached Aunty Ann's bed, swallowing hard.

'Hi, Aunty Ann,' I said quietly and she looked at me. I held her hand, told her that I loved her and thanked her for everything she had done for me. Aunty Ann continued to stare at me, glassy eyed and I guessed it was the diamorphine.

I tried to juggle being at Mum's bedside 280 miles away, visiting my aunt and delivering training and assessing staff in older people's services for work. It was not easy. Five days after she had been admitted, I went up to the ward to see Aunty Ann and a nurse politely motioned me to step outside the door to a side room. She had a look of sympathy on her face. She asked who I was and I told her. She then knocked on the door, and when one of my cousins said 'Come in', opened it for me to enter. My lovely aunt was lying in bed, eyes closed, with two of my cousins by her side. I leant against the wall, not knowing what to say.

My cousins and I made small talk. The cousin who was holding Aunty Ann's hand then asked me if would take over whilst they went out for a break. I talked to Aunty Ann, again saying how much I loved her. I stroked her hand. She was very poorly and not responding, though she was still breathing.

Then Aunty Ann's body gave a groan and when I checked her pulse there wasn't one. She had gone. My cousins came back into the room not long after. We were all deeply upset. Someone we had all loved so much had now left us.

The pain of losing Aunty Ann and the worry about what was happening to Mum were almost too much to bear. It seemed as though everything was going disastrously wrong at the same time. The family met at the hospital. We hugged each other as we visited Aunty Ann in the chapel of rest. At her funeral the service paid tribute to a wonderful lady who put everyone before herself.

After the service my brother, sister and I joined our cousins in the limousine to the crematorium. A young boy in a car in the outer lane raised his hat to us.

I had chocolate in my bag and offered it around.

I do not recall the next few days; oblivion accompanied by pain – lots of pain.

. . . .

If you experience a bereavement at a time when it is difficult to take a break:

- Take some time out, even if it is very brief; you need to clear your mind.
- Allow yourself to grieve.
- Talk about the good times with those who remember the person you have lost.
- Embrace the happy memories, they are so special and you can take them everywhere with you.

Chapter 8

Not being heard

I was tired. So tired. I felt it as I got off the tube and onto the train, and again as I got off the train to go and see Mum in hospital again. She had been there now for about two months and I had lost count of how many trips I had made to see her. I got the taxi to wait for me as I dropped my stuff off at the B&B so that it could take me on to the hospital. I really wanted to go to bed, but it was not an option. I also wanted someone else to watch over Mum so I could have a break, but this wasn't an option this evening either.

I said 'Hello' to the staff as I saw them, all busy, seeing to patients.

Mum was lying on her side in bed. She was tired too.

'Evening, Mum,' I whispered as I stroked her hand.

I didn't stay long; we were both so tired.

When I arrived on the ward the next morning, Mum was looking out of the window. She commented on the sun coming through and how lucky she was to have a bed next to the window.

I showed her copies of my newly published workbooks. She was very pleased for me and, as a staff nurse approached the bed, said quietly, 'They could do with them here. Quick, put them away.' As I was doing so, the staff nurse saw the one entitled *Effective Communication*. She asked to have a look at it and when the Ward Sister approached the bed she showed her it.

There were silences between Mum and me while we stared out of the window onto the car park and the trees, sometimes interrupted by talk about our memories, which were lovely to recapture. Mum talked about what a good singer she had once been.

'I don't think your singing skills have been passed on to any of us, Mum,' I said and we both laughed.

'No, but all three of you have done well for yourselves.' I agreed; we had. All three of us children had become managers sometime during our careers.

Two nurses came to Mum's bed and asked if they could wash her.

'Course you can,' Mum replied and I sat on the seats outside the ward and tried to read the newspaper, but I was too tired. I gave up and went for a walk, to see the ducks and to get some fresh air.

After about 30 minutes I returned to the ward but the curtains were still round Mum's bed. As I turned to go back out, a nurse came from behind the curtain and said that Mum would be ready in about five minutes. She was cheerful; I was glad as it meant that she had been cheerful with Mum. I waited outside the ward for about 10 minutes before going back in. Mum had been turned on to her other side and she saw me as I approached the bed.

'Good wash, Mum?' I asked.

'Yes thanks, feel nice and fresh.'

'Would you like some of your perfume on?'

'If it's not too much trouble.'

'Nothing's too much trouble, Mum,' I told her and she held up her wrists. I sprayed both and she rubbed her them together before putting her right wrist to her nose and smelling it. I sprayed some in the air too, ensuring that it didn't go near the bed next door, in case the lady in that bed had an allergy.

I walked around to the other side of the bed to put the perfume on Mum's locker and when I looked back at Mum, she was snoozing. I went out to use the toilet. Walking back towards her bed, I heard Mum say, 'What are you doing?' When I got a bit closer I could see the healthcare assistant hovering above Mum's head with a pair of headphones.

'I'm putting the headphones onto your head,' she said as she did so.

'I don't want them on,' Mum said. I stayed watching, silently, in disbelief that this was happening.

'I'll put them on your head because you might want to listen to music later,' she said.

'No I won't,' Mum replied.

'I'll leave them on your head anyway,' said the nurse.

This nurse was clearly not listening. Either she did not know that I was behind her or if she did she did not care. I stepped forward and said, 'My mum does not want the headphones on her head.'

'But she might want them later,' she told me.

'You have already told Mum this and she has clearly told you that she will not,' I told her.

She did not give me eye contact or remove the headphones from Mum's head; she walked away, not saying anything.

'You alright, Mum?' I asked as I gently took the headphones off; they were quite tight on her head.

'I am now,' replied Mum.

I kept my feelings under control as I did not want to worry Mum, but really I wanted to explode at the nurse for not respecting or listening to my mother.

I kept Mum's spirits up by saying that I would find her a new home, one where she would be safe, and we discussed what colours she would like in her bedroom. It took a while for me to convince Mum that she would be safe in a new nursing home, but eventually she began to smile. She had not been this happy since being in the hospital. I turned away so she could not see the tears in my eyes.

Mum ate a little lunch and had a snooze afterwards.

I took time to ponder on why the nurse who was responsible for my mum's care ignored her, and me. Whenever I said anything she ignored me. It was as though I was not there. I took a break when the nurses came to turn Mum, and went downstairs.

Time was dragging on; all we needed was a social worker allocated to Mum so she could be discharged. I checked for texts and missed calls on my mobile. One of my NVQ candidates had texted: 'I've done the work you set me. Now answering the knowledge questions. Airshow tomorrow. Taking my young son on the train to Southend to see it. Yeay!'

'I wonder how the individuals at the nursing home will feel tomorrow hearing those bomber planes in the sky,' I texted back.

'Never thought about that. I'm on tomorrow so I'll ask them.'

'I'm sure it will bring back a lot of memories, sad and/or happy for some. Now switching off phone as going back onto the ward to be with my mum. Bye x'

Back on the ward Mum was sleeping so I sat quietly by her bed. I read the magazine and afterwards just stared around the ward, bored. I made a mental note to myself to get an MP3 player.

Two healthcare assistants were stripping and remaking the bed next to Mum. They looked happy. Later they came to Mum's bed and awoke her as she needed to be turned. They apologised for waking her.

I stared out of the window whilst the curtains were pulled around Mum's bed and she was turned. I heard a lot of happy banter going on between the nurses and Mum, and I smiled.

Mum's eating and drinking were still poor; she would only have a few spoonfuls of food or a few sips of a drink. She asked for a drink and I gave her one. I opened up Mum's file to record the drink and saw lots of forms in there, many not completed. I knew the nurses were not helping Mum to drink because the jug of water and the fruity drinks that I took in for her were left untouched. I wished I could stay with her every minute of every day, but I couldn't.

One cleaner in particular was very good in not only talking to Mum but also giving her a drink when she asked for one. All cleaners on this ward were thorough at their job, which also involved steam cleaning the beds, bed base and rails; and the ward was spotless.

Mum was saying that her chest hurt; the Ward Sister brought some peppermint in hot water for indigestion, which surprised me as she was hardly eating or drinking anything. I thought it was something more than indigestion.

'Mum had difficulty eating a soft bread roll,' I told the staff nurse as she came to the end of the bed with the drug trolley.

'I owe you an apology for the way I spoke to you on the telephone the other day,' she said.

'Oh, do you?' I asked.

'Yes, I may have come across as not caring.' I felt too exhausted properly to acknowledge her apology; one error after another!

'Mum had difficulty eating a soft bread roll,' I repeated.

'It's because her mouth is very dry as she is not drinking,' the staff nurse told me. She approached Mum and administered some liquid which she told me was because Mum had an infection in her mouth. When Mum opened her mouth her tongue was brown in colour.

'Could this could be why she's not eating and drinking?' I asked.

When the nurse said it could be, I asked why I hadn't been told about the mouth infection rather than having to put two and two together myself. The staff nurse moved her trolley to the next bed without answering.

I informed the doctor and staff nurses on different occasions that a pattern was forming in Mum's eating and drinking and that she was complaining of a pain in her chest. The doctor said Mum could be refusing food because she was depressed. I explained that I didn't think she was actually refusing food, more that she couldn't digest it. The doctor said that he would write Mum up for anti-depressants. He did not seem to be listening either.

In the afternoon Mum and I talked occasionally; at other times I sat there and watched others or I read. Mum snoozed on and off. I looked at my watch 'Ten minutes before she is due to be turned again,' I said to myself. Fifteen minutes later two nurses came to Mum's bed asking her if they could turn her. They were happy and chatty and I left to get some fresh air, feeling a quiver of emotion; happy emotion. What I had just seen had pleased me and I did not need to stop and look at the ducks. I walked along the path and around the car park to stretch my legs before sitting on the bench and texting my sister.

'Mum is just being turned so I've come out for a bit of fresh air.'

'How is she today?' Ann texted back.

'Okay. I've just left her laughing with the nurses.'

'That's good x'

'Now going back up to the ward x'

I sent various other texts before going back into the hospital, aware that my life was spent either with Mum or working. Working across the country was usually manageable as I had my free time, but now my free time was taken up with making sure Mum was okay in a hospital where the staff had a duty of care, but didn't appear consistently to be doing what that required.

As I turned the corner into Mum's bay, I wondered what I would be faced with, but it was all good. Mum was on her side and looked happy. This was such a relief. I moved the chair to the side she was facing and sat down directly in her eye line. After we had run out of things to chat about I moved the chair back a bit so Mum could see the ward.

The ward was nice, calm and relaxing until the patient a couple of beds down started shouting. The staff nurse talked loudly to her from the end of her bed. I didn't think the patient was hearing her as she continued raising her voice. I couldn't make out what she was saying. I thought she was probably confused and/or scared as if she didn't know where she was and what was happening. The nurses were very busy and didn't have time to sit with her, to comfort her. I looked at Mum; she was snoozing so I quietly got up from my chair and walked over to the patient who was shouting.

I approached her bed slowly and smiled when she looked at me. She was still shouting, but not clearly enough for me to understand. She had her left arm raised in the air and was waving it softly. I raised my arm to hers, slowly so I did not frighten her. I touched her hand and placed my fingers onto her veiny hand. The skin was very thin and not comfortable to touch, but I ignored this and stroked her hand. She looked at me and I told her it was okay, she was safe and, as soon as I said it, I knew I was lying, but what else could I say to her?

She brought her arm down and I softly and carefully held her hand. I looked at her facial expression for it to tell me if this was okay, and I thought it was as she stopped shouting. I stayed with her for some time, talking about the weather, and she was looking at me so I guessed she was listening. When she drifted off for a snooze, I put her hand onto the bed, pulled the cover over her chest and went back to sitting by Mum, who was still asleep. I looked around the ward, caught the eye of the patient opposite and smiled.

The staff nurse did her drug round at the same time as tea arrived. Mum didn't eat much of her food. I tried to encourage her to eat, but after a few mouthfuls she said she didn't want any more.

The evening was the same as other evenings; Mum drifted off to sleep and I sat by her bed. It was time to leave when I saw the night staff coming on duty. As I left the hospital I was really surprised to see the healthcare assistant who had shovelled food into Mum's mouth leaving at the same time. As a minimum I thought she should have been suspended whilst they clarified what she had done, and it had only been a short while since I had reported her. Even though I had complained, things were not improving. I wondered how much worse it must be for other patients who had no one to speak up for them.

I got a taxi to the train station to go back home to the east coast. I was glad that the train was due in five minutes. I *so* needed to sleep. As the train pulled out of the station I sat back and closed my eyes. I drifted into sleep against my will. It was very late and I didn't like travelling late at night; you never knew who was going to be on the train. Eventually I couldn't fight it any longer and I dreamt about what had happened on the ward that day.

Hours later, when at last I was snuggled up in my own bed, I was so tired but I could not sleep. I felt helpless and scared because I knew Mum wasn't safe in the hospital. And I had left her there. If only I lived just round the corner I could call in daily. I knew however much other people visited her, they would not notice the things I did, and they probably would not speak up either. It is a difficult thing to do..

I was next at the hospital seven days later. I saw the doctor come near Mum's bed and walked over to him.

'Mum hasn't been turned for over three hours,' I told him.

'I'll tell the staff,' he replied.

I took this opportunity to express my concerns to the doctor about how the staff were asking Mum if she wanted painkillers the wrong way. He said to have a word with them; they wouldn't mind. I explained that I was fed up with telling them. I was here for Mum and finding it exhausting ensuring the nurses gave Mum the care she should have. He said he would have a word with the staff.

Later, with Mum's agreement, a staff nurse inserted a tube down Mum's throat into her stomach so she could be fed that way. I was glad that something was being done and was hopeful that it would work.

When a staff nurse was demonstrating to a student how to do the feed, Mum said she felt sick. She explained it could be because Mum had not eaten a whole meal for a while and she was feeling bloated. Later, the Ward Sister came over to us and asked Mum how she was feeling. Mum replied, 'I feel rotten.'

I felt useless. I was trying to stop her coming to any harm by being there as much as I could, but I knew it was not enough.

In my head I wondered what training the nurses received to enable them to become qualified. Years before I would have known, but since the training had gone out to the universities I didn't. I rang the Nursing and Midwifery Council and was informed that it depended on the individual universities and what they offered on their courses.

I was also told that there was no standard or essential training that nursing auxiliaries had to complete; it depended on the individual hospital training plan. At that particular time, the National Minimum Standards, set under the Care Standards Act 2000 (published by the Department of Health) stated what training care-staff working in care or nursing homes had to complete, but there was no standard for healthcare assistants (or 'nursing auxiliaries') working in hospitals. Fortunately, this is at last being addressed with the implementation of 'Minimum training standards and code of conduct for healthcare support workers and adult social care workers in England'. The Code of Conduct promises that 'Following the guidance will give you reassurance that you are providing safe and compassionate care of a high standard and the confidence to challenge others who are not.' Both compassion and the challenging of poor practice had been sadly lacking as far as my mother was concerned.

The new Code also says that it will 'tell the public and people who use health and care services exactly what they should expect from Healthcare Support Workers and Adult Social

Care Workers in England.' (http://www.skillsforhealth.org. uk/workforce-transformation/code-of-conduct-and-national-minimum-training-stan/) This new development will help unqualified staff as it provides a set of clear standards, and it will also help anyone who has a loved one or friend receiving care to know what they can expect. It will go some way in helping to prevent what happened to my late mother, but staff also need to be supported. Without that, it will make no difference.

I got a call from a new Social Worker, Vera, who rang to introduce herself. I explained to her that although my brother was the next of kin, I would be the person who would look at new homes for Mum. Before I could go ahead with this, Vera told me that I would have to wait for a form to be completed by one of the ward staff and my sister had agreed to do this by telephone. More waiting and more paperwork, but it was a relief to have Vera the Social Worker in place, at last.

Chapter 9

Choosing a new nursing home

Early on, when my mother had been in hospital for only a short time, I had received a telephone call at 6.45 pm from Kay, Nurse Assessor from the hospital, stating that she would be visiting Mum to complete a Continuing Healthcare form and asking if I could be on the ward at 9 am the following morning to complete a form as next of kin. I had explained that I couldn't as it was too short notice given that I lived on the east coast. I had also pointed out that I was not the official next of kin. I had given her my brother's telephone number. My brother worked nights; he had been able to meet with Kay at a later time the next day and complete the form. So far, so good.

A few weeks later, I had heard from Kay again. She had informed me that Mum would be NHS-funded in a new nursing home, and she was fit to be discharged. She had told me that she would liaise with the brokerage team, and someone would contact me with a list of homes with vacancies

I didn't hear anything for quite a while and telephoned Kay to tell her this. Kay said she had sent the information on to the brokerage team. I asked her to follow it up as I was due to go to down in a few days' time and would incorporate a visit to possible nursing homes then. I said I would like to arrange the visits from my home where I had access to the Care Quality

Commission's website and could see the inspection reports of the homes. No lists arrived.

For my next visit I took the train. When I was walking into the train station to take the first of the series of trains down to the west coast, I caught a glimpse of white hair, white jumper and black trousers and for a second, I thought it was Aunty Ann. My heart was happy for those few seconds until logic reminded me that I must have made a mistake.

I checked in at the B&B before walking to the supermarket and getting some food. Then I took the bus to the hospital. As I entered the ward it was obvious that the nurses were expecting me. (I assumed the Discharge Officer had mentioned that I would be visiting.) Several staff rushed up to me and gave me information on how my mother had been. I found it overpowering. I had just completed a seven-and-a-half-hour train journey and was shattered.

One of the staff nurses told me that Mum had been unwell for the past 24 hours and had problems with her heart and respiration. Her blood pressure was low.

The Discharge Officer and the Ward Sister then came over to Mum's bed and told her that she was fit for discharge. This shocked me after the staff nurse had told me about her breathing and other problems. I was given a list of homes that had vacancies; I noticed this information was over six months old. I didn't say anything, but I knew I would have to go onto the Care Quality Commission website and look at the nursing homes myself. Given Mum's state of health, I was also wondering if it was worthwhile.

Back at the B&B I made myself a cup of tea and booted up the laptop. I typed 'Care Quality Commission' in the search bar and the website came up. I clicked on 'nursing homes' and tapped in the postcode of the areas I wanted to look at.

There were lots of homes and I refined my search. My brother wanted Mum to live no more than 20 minutes away from him. I had told him that it would depend on the standard of the home and what it offered and, of course, if it had a vacancy.

Reading some of the CQC inspection reports about the homes and their star ratings made me cry: 'older people are left in soiled bedding', 'older people do not have a choice on when to get up and go to bed', and so on. One report made me very angry and I rang the company's head office in London.

'I'm just on the internet looking at suitable homes for my mother and I see one of yours on there.'

'If you hold the line I'll put you through.'

'Thank you,' I replied.

'Hello, can I help you?'

'Yes, I'm on the CQC website looking at suitable homes for my mum and I've just read a report on one of your homes.'

'Oh yes. Do you like it?' she asked.

'No I don't, actually. The reason I'm ringing is to say I'm appalled that your organisation has let one of its homes get into this state. Your website and your ad on TV are very misleading.'

'I'm really sorry. Please give me the name of the home and I will discuss it with the director.'

I gave her the details and ended the call. I was fuming!

I went out for a walk and tried to clear my head. How could things like that happen to older people? Older people who were vulnerable.

Once I was back on the east coast, Vera, the Social Worker, rang and asked if I had had a look at some homes. I told her Mum was not well. She said she did not know this and would visit the ward. She rang back to say that Mum was not fit for discharge at the moment, and she would review her in two weeks' time. She advised that I should still look at possible homes.

Later, I rang the hospital to speak to the Discharge Officer, again, to ask if I should still go and visit homes, bearing in mind that Mum's health was not too good. The Discharge Officer I had been dealing with was on annual leave and I spoke to someone else in her office who advised me still to go ahead. I asked her if she was sure, and she repeated that I should still look at homes. I informed her that I would be down again for a few days and would look at homes whilst I was there.

The next thing was to call the brokerage team to try to get up-to-date information. 'If you give me your email address, I'll send you details of nursing homes that have current vacancies,' my contact there told me.

I gave her my email address and asked, 'Are you going to ask me why Mum is in hospital with a broken tibia on one side and a fractured femur on the other side? And why I am looking for a new home for her?'

'I suppose I should,' she replied. 'I'll take it up with the home.'

She emailed me some addresses of homes that had vacancies the next evening. I looked at the CQC reports and rang the homes to make arrangements to go and see them.

Everything kept changing. I received a call from Vera, the Social Worker, telling me that Mum's care would be funded by the NHS and not social services. Because of this, Vera told me, she would not be able to be involved. I was not happy about this as it would leave Mum vulnerable again. It had not been easy acknowledging that Mum was at risk, being in the profession myself, but the chain of events we had been through had forced me to do so.

Back on the west coast, I spent most of the morning with Mum. She wasn't voluntarily making conversation, but answered when I spoke to her and we talked. I told her that I was going to look at some new homes for her, and she was happy about that. The nurses knew where I was going and, as I used the disinfectant alcohol gel on my hands near the door, they wished me luck. I was emotional and squeaked a 'Thank you'. It would be such a big improvement to get Mum out of the hospital now.

I went down the stairs and took time out looking at the ducks. I rested my head against the wall and could have happily fallen asleep there. But I got myself together, took a deep breath and walked across to the bus stop, which was strangely comforting in its familiarity.

On the train to the area where my brother lived, I received a message on my mobile voicemail from the Ward Sister to ask if I could pop in and see her that morning as they wanted to move Mum to a different ward. I telephoned my sister.

'Can you ring the Ward Sister and tell her that I've already been on the ward this morning, and that I'd like to have been with Mum when they move her to another ward so that I could have done the handover?'

'Why are they moving her?' Ann asked.

'They're having single-sex wards now, so all women need to be moved this afternoon. Had I known this before getting the train I would have stayed with Mum to do the changeover myself.'

Some time later I received a text from Ann.

'I rang the hospital and the Ward Sister says she is doing the move this afternoon. She also told me that the feeding tube had been stopped and Mum is going for an x-ray to see if the tube is in the correct position. XX.'

I replied, 'Let's hope it is. XX'

I put the phone in my pocket, sat back in my seat and closed my eyes; they stung a little from being so tired. The rocking motion of the train sent me to sleep for a short time, then I realised the train had stopped for longer than it should. I opened my eyes: we were at a train station and the police were there, escorting two youths off the train. I wondered what they had done.

*

I saw various nursing homes. Some were nicely decorated, some needed to be decorated, but I realised that Mum would be in bed for some time yet, until the grade 4 pressure sore was healed, so the bedroom and the staff values and attitudes were the most important things I needed to consider. I felt emotional knowing that Mum would spend a long time in her new bedroom.

The first home was very nice, very well decorated and well looked after. Some individuals were in an activity session with a staff member. I liked this, although I knew Mum could not attend any sessions as she would be lying in bed, on her side, whilst her pressure sore healed, if it ever did. I asked if staff went in to read to individuals or chat apart from to do personal care and so on. She said they did.

My note to myself about this home was: 'Too clean and tidy. Nothing out of place. Not sure what time is given to the individuals in the home who do not or cannot participate in activity sessions.'

The second home was quite different. I walked into the reception area and a reek of urine hit me. I waited at reception for a while, until two members of staff who were laughing came to ask what I wanted. I explained who I was and that I had an appointment booked to look around the home. They took a while to decide who would show me around. I was not impressed with their attitudes, nor the strong stench of urine that filled the air everywhere as we looked around. It was so strong I almost rushed into a bedroom to open the window for some fresh air.

Some bedroom doors were open and I couldn't help but have a quick look and saw the used sheets were on the bedroom floor in some of them. In another bedroom a man saw us pass his door and called out. I stopped in my tracks expecting the member of staff showing me round to go and see what he wanted, but she didn't.

'I'm happy to wait here whilst you see to the gentleman,' I told her.

'Nah, he'll be quiet in a minute,' she replied.

I was shocked, but tried not to show it.

'I'll stay here whilst you go and see him.' I told her with raised eyebrows.

She went in to see him and I stayed in the corridor, wishing there was a window from which I could inhale some clean air. The odour of urine was awful.

We continued our walk around the home and the staff member did not appear affected by the smell. 'She must be used to it,' I thought. I did not see any other members of staff and wondered if they were all busy, or skiving. I found it hard to ask any questions as I knew Mum would not be living here and I felt sorry for the people who were. I told myself that I would report this home to the Care Quality Commission when I got a chance, as no home should smell like that.

My note to myself about this second home was: 'Didn't like the attitude of the staff member showing me around. Something was terribly wrong for a home to smell that strongly of urine. Were people not being taken to the toilet, washed or changed?'

The third home was the only home with a vacancy near to where my brother lived. The décor of this house was okay, though not as good as the first home, and with wear and tear such as wheelchair marks on the doors, which showed it was used. The staff were rushing about, but I could tell it was not put on for my benefit. They were genuinely busy supporting individuals. I took a look around with the Manager and she asked one woman if she would like to show me her bedroom and explained why. The woman agreed and we went into her bedroom. She voluntarily told me how she felt about leaving her home a few months before and moving in here. Whilst she talked I could hear another member of staff walking by with an individual and it all sounded pleasant.

I continued to walk around the home and to question the Manager and I liked what I was hearing and seeing. I would be happy for Mum to have a room here. The room could be decorated as she chose, and, as well as staff going into residents' rooms to do personal care, they also had dedicated time where staff members went to sit with the residents who were bedridden and read, talk, or just provide company.

My note to myself was very simple: 'I want Mum to move in here.'

Still, I had made an appointment to see another, so I then visited a fourth home. This was clean and well decorated, but it had too many hallways and they sloped. How this had been allowed to happen I didn't know. How could older people who have difficulty walking, walk on a slope? The hallways were of vinyl, easy to clean, but slippery for people to walk on. The TV was blaring out in the lounge and no one was in there; everyone was in the dining room eating their tea. The residents wore bibs and some had baby mugs with their drink in them. I wondered why they didn't use napkins instead of bibs, and whether they preferred a straw and a glass instead of a baby mug.

I was shown round the house and found it too clinical; it was not personalised. The Manager told me that the individuals liked going out into the garden. I looked out of the window and saw the steep back garden and wondered how they managed to get out there, and, if they did go out there, how they stopped themselves from falling down the steep slope.

When the individuals living in the home had finished eating they were taken to the lounge; not one was asked if they wanted to go there. Some were left in the dining area for no apparent reason. I asked the Manager if they could be helped to go out of the dining room. She arranged for staff to do this. When the last individual had been moved out a member of staff put a CD into the machine and turned it up really loud. 'Bless 'em all. Bless 'em all,' she said. I was not impressed.

At the end of the visit, I passed the lounge and many individuals were sitting in chairs looking at the TV, some with tables in front of them. Nothing was on them and I wondered was this for later, for when they had a drink, or was it to stop the residents getting up and walking about? If it was the latter then it was, and still is, illegal as it is restraint.

I felt pressure from the manager for me to move Mum into this home. I explained that it was not what I was looking for and went through all the negatives I had observed.

My note to myself here was depressing: 'No positive interaction between the staff and the people they should be supporting. The only interaction I saw was task orientated – i.e. moved individuals from one area to the next.'

. . . .

What you may need to know about moving a vulnerable person from a hospital to a care/nursing home:

- The hospital should assign a Social Worker to the individual.
- The Social Worker will compile an assessment to ascertain what care the individual will need – for example, nursing care in a nursing home; 24-hour care in a care home; care at home with support going in.
- The assessment will show whether the individual needs social care or continued nursing care when they leave hospital. If it is the latter, the NHS will cover the cost.
- If you have been assessed as needing social care, your Social Worker can refer to the hospital's brokerage team on your behalf; otherwise, you can contact the team yourself. The hospital's brokerage team can find service providers who can meet your needs and choices and give information about these (for example, costs of the service, registration details, star ratings, whether the provider can meet your specific preferences).

Chapter 10

Hospital care continues to deteriorate

I visited Mum as soon as I got off the train. I walked into the ward that she had been moved to and looked around. A health-care assistant asked who I had come to see. I told her and she replied, 'Okay. I'll shout at your mum and tell her you're here.' She smiled and went off to see Mum. I smiled back. I knew that she had not meant what she had said; she had just got the words mixed up a bit. She came back to me and as she took me over to where Mum was, she apologised for getting her words wrong; she said she was from Somalia. I didn't know then that this healthcare assistant would turn out to be the most compassion-ate member of staff we would encounter, but that I would only see her on this one occasion.

Mum was lying down on her back in the bed. I asked the staff nurse who was on duty if she should be lying in that position as she had been propped up since her admission in March, some 11 weeks earlier, so that nothing got onto her chest. I was also concerned that as she had been upright for some time, lying flat could cause pain because her muscles were not used to it. The staff nurse said Mum would be alright.

Mum asked for a drink and I asked a different staff nurse for a jug of water. She said Mum could not have any as she was to have 'nil by mouth' until they received the results of the X-ray to see if the feeding tube was in the right place. As Mum was desperate for a drink, I insisted the nurse ask the doctor if Mum could go back onto fluids and food. She paged him and said he would be up later as he was in theatre. The doctor came up about an hour and a half later and told me that Mum could go back on to fluids and food and that the X-ray was clear.

Mum's temperature dropped and a staff nurse put a 'blower blanket' over her to warm her up. (A blower blanket is an inflatable covering, a bit like a lilo, that can be filled with warm air.) Unfortunately they left it on too long and Mum overheated. Could they get nothing right? I took a deep breath and said within, 'Another error!'

I could see Mum was not well and I sat quietly by her bed. Now and again she would open her eyes to see if I was there, and would smile and close her eyes again.

For the first time a student nurse came over and did a pain assessment: 'On a score of 0 to 10, how much pain are you in; has the pain worsened or got better...?' It was good this was being done, but it should have been happening on a regular basis on the other ward Mum had been on as well.

Trying to organise Mum's locker, I found the satsumas and grapes we had bought her three weeks before in an inside drawer, along with a letter and batteries for a hearing aid for a different patient. I took a break and went for a walk. I stared at the ducks, unblinking, watching, totally shattered.

Back on the ward, a different staff nurse approached Mum's bed and said she would do a test to aspirate the naso-gastric tube through which Mum was being fed; if it showed stomach acid, then the tube was in the right position; if it didn't, then we would have to assume it was in the wrong place.

The staff on this ward had a very cold approach towards the patients, apart from the healthcare assistant from Somalia. The other unregistered staff on shift were very task-orientated and did not engage with any of the patients.

There was little room to manoeuvre and sit around Mum's bed. I had to sit behind the blood pressure machine which stopped me from being able see her. There were also too many leads around my feet. I expressed my concerns to a healthcare assistant, but nothing was done.

Many buzzers were going off but an unregistered nurse and a student nurse tutted to each other and walked away. I went to see what the patients wanted; I could only help with getting them the commode or their glasses, but at least I could do something.

Mum was very sleepy and I held her hand as I sat by her bed.

The next morning I walked over to Mum's bed and noticed that she looked shattered. I also noticed she did not have a jug of water. I approached a staff nurse.

'My mother hasn't got any water by her bed.'

'She can't have any. She's nil by mouth,' I was told.

'The doctor told me yesterday that Mum could go back onto food and fluids.'

'Well, he didn't tell us.'

'You mean to tell me that Mum hasn't been given food or drink since yesterday morning?'

'I can't do anything until the doctor tells me,' the staff nurse replied.

'I understand, but the doctor told me that Mum could have food and fluids. She's desperate for a drink and she's already lost a lot of weight since admission to the other ward.'

'Sorry, I can't do anything until I hear from the doctor.'

In fury and frustration I wanted to punch her. My poor mother... I did my best to keep my temper.

'Please bleep the doctor immediately. There are three health-care assistants on this morning who were here last night, and one of them brought Mum a jug of water then. Why haven't they noticed that she's not been given a drink?'

The staff nurse did not answer.

She came back later and said that she had contacted the doctor and Mum could have food and fluids. This was a relief to hear. I poured some water for Mum and she drank quite a bit. The feed tube was not in position anymore; the staff nurse said the staff had tried to insert it again, but the aspiration test did not show stomach acid so it wasn't in the right place.

There was a pile of cards on the bedside cabinet. I opened the envelopes. 'Happy birthday, Mum,' I said and read out the messages to her. Mum wasn't well enough to acknowledge, let alone celebrate, her birthday.

Later I asked the same staff nurse something more about Mum's care and she responded by saying that, 'Your mum has only been with us for one and a half days. We're still trying to get to know her.' I explained that she had been in the hospital since March, and that the handover from the previous ward sister and her notes should help.

Totally upset and frustrated I went downstairs and knocked on the office door of the Patient Advisory Liaison Service (PALS) to express my concerns. There was no answer. I went back up to the ward. Later I went back down to the PALS office again and they still were not there. I asked at reception how I could speak to someone and they directed me to a room opposite the toilets. When I got there I found it was the Bereavement office.

On the way back up to the ward, I stopped to gaze at the notice board. My eyes caught a flyer which read:

> 'Person-centred care for older people.
> Dignity… we deserve it!
> Make sure we get it!'

It had contact details for the 'Matron for Older Persons & Stroke', including her email address. I copied down the details so I could contact her and ask if dignity could be provided for my mother as well as for those who had had a stroke.

71

I left the ward at lunchtime and got a taxi to the train station, ready to start my journey home. I didn't want to leave, but my niece and my brother would be going in later and I had had a long conversation with my niece, telling her everything that had happened and what I wanted her to watch out for. She worked in social and health care too.

I received a text from her while I was travelling: 'The nasogastric tube was inserted and placed incorrectly. Tube was blocked as it had not been flushed. Tube removed. Nan nil by mouth. xx'

I texted back: 'Thanks. Let's hope they get it sorted soon. xx'

I arrived home at 10.20 pm. I was too tired to eat, but knew that I had to boot up the computer and check my emails, especially my work ones. First, though, I unpacked my trolley case and loaded the washing machine.

The amount of charge in my mobile was low so I turned it off and decided to charge it up the following morning. I'd never liked to charge it during the night after reading that battery chargers can catch fire if left for a long time. I threw the mobile charger into its usual corner of the kitchen a little too hard and it bounced back off the wall. I realised my nerves felt raw. Very wearily I went and unlocked the study and booted up the computer.

. . . .

What to look out for when someone is moved within or between hospitals:

- Try to have someone with you if it is you who are being moved; try to be with your loved one when he or she is moved – but, as my story shows, this can be very difficult.
- Ask questions of the nurses and the doctors.
- Find out if the routines (meal times, visits by doctors, drug rounds) are different.
- Ask if you can stay and help your relative with their food, if your support is needed.

Chapter 11

Shocking news

The following morning – a Sunday, 11½ weeks after Mum was first admitted – my sister rang the ward at 9.15 am and was told that Mum was: 'Sleepy, blood sugar OK, comfortable, no pain.' Ann told me that she was going to go down the following day. I said I didn't think I could as I'd only just got back and was shattered, not only because of the seven-and-a-half-hour train journey, but also from the emotional strain. It was good to know that Ann would be seeing Mum.

A little later that same morning, my brother rang Ann and me individually; he was at the hospital and he said the doctor had asked to see him later. He said that the doctor wanted to talk to him as Mum wasn't getting better. He asked me what I wanted him to do if the doctor told him that Mum only had a short time to live. Though I was well aware that Mum was very ill, it was a terrible shock to be asked this question. Nothing I had seen the day before had prepared me for it.

Keith asked if I wanted him to tell me as soon as he knew the worst, or to tell me after she had passed away. He was very brave, but I cried. I apologised for crying and through the tears I said I wanted to know. He said he needed to go, which made me think that he wanted to shed a tear too.

No more than two hours after my sister's call to the ward, my brother rang her again, this time to say we needed to get down to the hospital as soon as we could. We threw our stuff into bags and started out. I say bags, I only had one small bag with toiletries and undies in it. In my haste I accidentally left my mobile charger where it had fallen on the kitchen floor – so unlike me, as I often worked away and packed what I needed on autopilot.

My sister drove and we talked sheer nonsense all the way there. When we did accidentally touch on the subject of Mum, we quickly changed it because we knew that if we didn't we would break down. It was important that my sister focused on the road and I kept her focused. Whilst Ann drove, I rang through to our usual B&B; unfortunately they were booked up. I rang another one and they were fully booked too. Having somewhere to stay wasn't our priority; Mum was. We would find a B&B when we got there, and if they were all full, we'd sleep on the beach. We didn't really care.

We arrived and agreed we would stock up on food and soft drinks for all of us later. We didn't know how long we would be with Mum but we were adamant we would stay with her until…

We parked the car in the car park and ran across to the entrance and then through the double door to the stairs, dodging people who were in our way and grabbing a squirt of alcohol gel on our hands before going into the ward.

Everything had changed. We found that Mum had been moved into a side room and had been put on to something called the 'Liverpool Pathway'. We introduced ourselves to the staff nurse at the desk and asked what the 'Liverpool Pathway' was. I assumed she would take us into a side room and tell us privately, but she didn't. She told us there at reception, and as matter of factly as if we had been discussing the weather.

'The correct term is the Liverpool Care Pathway. It enables the patient to die free of pain and with dignity and respect.'

I had only left the hospital the afternoon of the day before with no inkling that Mum was dying, though I could see that she was very poorly. Nobody had said anything; they had just let me go. I had made the seven-our train journey home and now here I was, back again.

'When was it decided that Mum should go into a side room?' I whispered to my brother. He had been called in to see the doctor early that morning and, as they were discussing Mum's care, the Ward Sister had said, 'I have the room ready.' That indicated that they had known the stage Mum was at yesterday, but they hadn't told me, or even Ann when she'd rung that morning.

Keith shrugged his shoulders.

'What did they say in the meeting?' I asked him.

He said the doctor had explained that they could continue with the treatment for the pressure sore, turning every few hours and re-dressing the wound, but with no guarantee of Mum getting through it, or make Mum comfortable, with no pain, and put her on the 'Liverpool Care Pathway' so she could pass away with dignity and respect. He had chosen the second option.

'You did the right thing,' I told him, and I hugged him. What a devastating decision to have to make. What would I have done in his place? I could barely think. I was like an exhausted robot!

'Dignity and respect... there's been no dignity or respect,' I muttered to myself, aware that this wasn't the time to start moaning.

After that, we took it in turns to go for loo or meal breaks. My brother was a night worker and he opted to do the nights and my sister and I the days, although trying to get Keith to go and have a break during the day was a hard task. He had a camper van, so for the next three days he was able to sleep in that in the car park. The evening staff were good to him, offering him cake and drinks. We rarely got offered anything during the day, unless we caught the tea trolley when it was doing its rounds. Keith's daughter, Vic, also spent as much time at the hospital as she could.

On one occasion on that first day, I came out of Mum's room and popped downstairs for a bit of fresh air. I stopped to look at the ducks, which gave me time to collect my thoughts. I gazed into the pond to see the little ducklings following their mother. They were pretty and so lucky to have a mother. Then I felt guilty for taking 'time out' and went back upstairs to be with Mum and the family.

When I went back into Mum's room I turned my head to the right before going in and said 'Hello' to an older lady who was also in her own room. She told me that she lived by herself and had fallen over. Luckily no bones were broken. Her neighbour would be popping in later. She asked about Mum, and I started blubbing. I couldn't help it, and I couldn't believe it when she told me sharply, 'Pull yourself together; it happens to all of us.'

I wanted to text people to tell them what was happening, but I realised I had left my charger at home. I felt cut off from the outside world.

While Mum was on the Liverpool Pathway we ensured one of us was with her round the clock and tried to go for breaks in pairs. The nearby pub did lovely steaks and two meals for the price of one. It also meant that we each had a good half-an-hour break once each day, which was important in keeping our stress at bay.

On that first day in the side room (it was still Sunday), when the nurses came into the room to say they were going to wash and turn Mum, we realised none of us had had a meal break and decided all four of us – Keith, Vic, Ann and me – should go out together whilst Mum was washed.

'Mum, we're off to get something to eat. See you later,' my brother said, and in unison we said, 'See you later, Mum.'

Just as we were leaving the room a nurse came and said that she wanted to change the machine at the end of the bed. She unplugged it and took the machine away. We did not know if it was a machine Mum needed or if it had been used by the previous patient and left there. It was very quiet, so quiet we had not realised it was on, if indeed it was. As ever, nothing was explained to us.

It was nice for the four of us, two sisters, brother and niece, to be together and chat about things that we couldn't talk about in front of Mum.

When we got back, Mum was lying on her back and screaming in pain. It was a high pitched desperate scream that went right through me. She was screaming, 'Do something! Do something!'

Fighting back the tears we asked, 'What do you want us to do, Mum?'

'Anything. Just do it, p-l-e-a-s-e!' she begged.

We called for help and the nurses turned Mum onto her side. The two who had washed and turned her had put her on her back and the catheter was pressing into her grade 4 pressure sore. They must also have dislodged the pipe that was blowing air into her mattress as later that evening the mattress went flat and she was squashed up.

I later mentioned this to a staff nurse, who said that it was probably the cleaners unplugging it and not putting the plug back in. 'They do that occasionally.' I told her that the cleaners that day had not unplugged anything as we had been in the room when the cleaning was done. There was no apology or compassion from this nurse.

Later that same evening, my sister and I visited various B&Bs until we found one with two vacancies. We explained that we wanted to stay a few nights but that our mother was very ill at the hospital and we couldn't be sure how long we would need to be there. The owner read our faces and seemed to understand what was happening.

'Pay me for the few nights and we can discuss more if you need them,' she said. We appreciated her kindness during this difficult time, and thanked her.

What you may need to know about the Liverpool Care Pathway

The 'Liverpool Care Pathway for the Dying Patient', to give it its full name, covers palliative care options for patients in the final days or hours of life and was formulated to help doctors and nurses provide quality end-of-life care. It was developed in the late 1990s for the care of terminally ill cancer patients, but was then extended to include all patients deemed to be dying. The intention behind the Pathway's development was to provide a 'joining up' of the multi-disciplinary team (doctors, nurses etc) in discontinuing medical treatment and providing good palliative care during the last days and hours of a patient's life.

Before a patient is put on the Pathway, the multi-disciplinary team caring for her/him must agree that all reversible causes for her/his condition have been considered and that s/he really is 'dying'. They must then decide what palliative care is appropriate and what treatments should be stopped to allow the patient to die with as much dignity and as little pain as possible.

Since its introduction, the Pathway has, however, proved controversial, or rather its use has, and its implementation has come in for considerable criticism. This has largely been because decisions to put patients on the Pathway have been taken at ward level, without an appropriate doctor being involved, and without patients and families being consulted or even informed.

Even worse, on 25 October 2012 the *Daily Mail* reported some particularly worrying claims relating to the Pathway – that hospitals have been paid in excess of £30 million to hit targets for the number of patients dying on the Pathway and that those targets require between a third and two thirds of patients who die on their wards to do so on the Pathway. (www.dailymail.co.uk/news/article-2223286/Hospitals-bribed-patients-pathway-death-Cash-incentive-NHS-trusts-meet-targets-Liverpool-Care-Pathway.html#ixzz2KXF9743O.)

Critics claim that while the Pathway is intended to ease the final hours for patients who are close to death and to spare them from interventions that cannot help, it is being used as a way of hastening the deaths of terminally ill patients by withdrawing life-saving treatment. Patients are sedated and denied nutrition and fluids and, the *Mail* reported, 'on average any patient put on the Pathway dies within 29 hours.'

I am pleased to say that the Association for Palliative Medicine, which represents doctors working in hospices and on specialist hospital wards, subsequently organised an inquiry into the Pathway. I shared my late mother's experiences of being on it with the inquiry. The outcome is that the use of the Liverpool Care Pathway should be phased out within the next six to 12 months and replaced with an end-of-life care plan. On 16 July 2013, new guidance was given to doctors and nurses caring for people in the last days of life; you can read this in full here: www.ncpc.org.uk/sites/default/files/Guidance_for_doctors_and_nurses%20_Liverpool_Care_Pathway.pdf

If someone you care for is put on the Liverpool Care Pathway:
- Ask which health professionals caring for your loved one have been involved in making that decision and request an opportunity to discuss the decision with them; in particular make sure that a doctor was involved.
- Ask to see the Liverpool Care Pathway care plan for your loved one and what is to be delivered as palliative care.
- Ask for support for yourself and the person who is dying, from the palliative care team.
- Consider if the person who is dying would prefer to be moved to a hospice or die at home.

And remember:
- Never accept care you are not happy with.
- Say what you want to happen.
- Express how you feel.
- Do not let the system drag you down.

Chapter 12

Two days before Mum leaves us

My sister and I met for breakfast. We didn't ask how the other was feeling or had slept because we knew the answer. It was as though we were robots, automatically doing different tasks, feeling empty. At breakfast I could see that I was by far the youngest person staying... They played some songs from Mum's era, which brought back memories I couldn't cope with. I panicked and ran to the loo. I didn't want to cry in the dining room and spoil everyone's breakfast.

I did manage to eat some breakfast but couldn't taste anything. We had lost Aunty Ann only seven weeks before and now we were going to lose Mum any day. It hurt so badly.

We went to the supermarket to buy more food and drink, and a battery charger for my mobile. I needed to share my thoughts and feelings with people outside of the immediate family.

Ann and I arrived at the hospital, did the usual hand cleaning and said hello to Mum and Keith. Shortly afterwards our niece, Vic, arrived. She was a breath of fresh air, always chirpy and smiling. We encouraged Keith to go and take a break, which, after a lot of persuasion, he did. We made small talk in Mum's room: we laughed, we fell silent, we nearly cried and then we ate; we laughed, then we chatted and fell silent; and this continued.

Mum was dying. They were giving her drugs just to keep her comfortable and reduce her pain. All I wanted was for her not to suffer any more. Only two months before she had had a discharge date of 8 April. It seemed extraordinary now. That date had come and gone; she had not been discharged because there had been no Social Worker in place, at the time, to manage the process. We would never find out why.

Only the week before I had looked around those nursing homes, and chosen the one I wanted Mum to move into. Not so long before Mum had been very much alive. Why was she now dying?

It was rare for the staff on this ward to speak to us, but their irritation was obvious. Their facial expressions and body language said it all.

On one occasion when we had left the room whilst the nurses washed and turned Mum, and we were waiting just outside the door by reception, I heard a doctor, with a group of what looked like medical students around him, refer to 'a nutty patient'. Although this was not Mum's doctor, and it was not aimed at her, it was really bad to hear this from a professional, especially one who was teaching young doctors.

We went back into Mum's room when the nurses came out, and staff continued to come in without knocking. There seemed to be little dignity, sympathy or compassion for Mum, or for us as a family. On one occasion when a staff nurse came in without knocking, my sister asked, 'Please, is Mum really dying?' Of course she knew the answer, but she hoped to get some reaction, or some apology for barging in with so little regard for how we might all be feeling. The staff nurse carried on doing what she had come in to do with no acknowledgement of any of us, or of what my sister has asked.

Mum suddenly 'awoke' saying strange things and was hysterical. We all jumped up from our seats in shock. As time went on she kept saying, 'Do something!' When we asked her what she wanted us to do she pitifully said, 'I don't know.' We did not know what to do. We tried to eliminate things that could be causing her pain and, on checking the morphine driver under her pillow that was designed to keep her free from pain and slightly sedated, found it was empty. Mum had not had the morphine she needed to control her pain and let her die with dignity. The hospital couldn't even get this right.

I told the staff nurse that the morphine driver was empty. We waited ages. Then I told a doctor. His only response was that Mum's pressure sore was looking better. This seemed completely inconsistent with Mum being on the Liverpool Pathway and did nothing to help with Mum's pain relief.

My brother, sister and niece tried comforting Mum by holding her. She continued to shout in pain and then she called my name. Quickly I brushed the tears away and said, 'I'm here, Mum,' and joined the hug. Her body seemed to relax a little and she appeared to be less anxious. Whilst we tried to comfort her, we told her she could let go, in case she was holding onto life for our sakes; that it would be okay and we would be okay.

As the day went on, we learnt there was no morphine on the ward and staff had to wait to get it from the pharmacy. One and a half hours later, a staff nurse came in and said, 'Gosh, it's hot in here.' There was no compassion for our grief, no understanding that we were trying to reassure and release Mum. She put the morphine in the driver and left the room without any apology for the wait. Regulations demand that two nurses should be present when administering a controlled drug, but she acted by herself.

What would have happened if we had not been there? I wondered. And how many other older people were treated like this? How many of them had no one with them to keep the staff from hurting them? Being with my family in the room was comforting, and gave us a sense of solidarity.

A male student nurse came into Mum's room to wash her. We left the room and stayed outside the door. He came out and asked an unregistered nurse to help him turn Mum. She said she would when she had finished what she was doing. As he went back into the room I saw through the door opening that the bedding was not covering Mum's thigh area. There was a loose fitting cloth covering the private area, which I assumed was to preserve her dignity, but the lower part of her body was exposed and on show. The door was now closed and I looked through the small window. He was staring down at her thighs. I went in.

'I know you're waiting for the nurse to help you, but please pull the sheet over my mother's lower half and show her some respect,' I demanded, pulling it over as I spoke. He stared at me, said nothing, offering no apology. I walked out of the door and closed it behind me. I looked through the small window again and saw him spray some of Mum's perfume around her neck; a nice gesture, but he then patted her neck as men do after they have applied aftershave. This was a student nurse who one day might qualify to become a registered nurse and possibly go on to manage a ward. What had he learned and who was his tutor that he couldn't even get the basics right, I asked myself.

A nurse came in and changed the VAC (Vacuum Assisted Closure) machine, an airtight seal over the pressure sore which sucked the serum fluid or blood from the infected area. This treatment had not been offered before the move to end-of-life care. Only now that Mum was dying did we learn it was available.

Mum was having problems breathing and a healthcare assistant came in to put a mask on her. When she had finished we asked her if she could put some gauze on Mum's nose to stop the oxygen mask rubbing and causing a blister. Her response was cold and detached, as it always was. She had been flirting with a male nurse on the first evening Mum was brought to this ward and cussed when the patients pressed their buzzers. She got some gauze and put it incompetently on Mum's nose with the corners of it sticking out and very close to Mum's eyes.

'Can you cut the gauze so my mother won't panic if she wakes and sees the corners of the gauze?' I asked.

'I haven't got any scissors with me,' she replied.

My niece and I looked at each other and I said, 'Well, we haven't either. Can't you go and get some?'

'They're in my locker,' she replied, not about to leave and get them.

'Well, can you go and get them, please?' my niece asked. Without saying anything she reluctantly left the room.

'Do you think she's going to get them?' my niece asked.

'Let's hope so,' I replied.

My brother and sister came back from their break. We all looked towards the door as the healthcare assistant walked in without knocking, trimmed the gauze and walked out again without a word. In unison, my niece and I said, 'Thank you.'

I visited the Bereavement Office with my sister. We asked for information on the Liverpool Pathway. They did not have any. Fortunately my brother had his laptop with him and found a description on the internet.

What we gathered was that the 'Liverpool Care Pathway' was a *planned* 'journey' for people to end their lives in a dignified way. If the hospital had planned Mum's departure, they would surely have had morphine in stock, staff trained in end-of-life care and referred us to the Palliative Care team, from whom we would have got some support.

Back on the ward, we continued taking it in turns to pop downstairs for a loo break, fresh air and phone calls. As I walked down the stairs, two female volunteers from a different ward, who had just helped with feeding, were expressing concern about staff ignoring patients on the ward.

We asked ourselves why Mum was holding on. Was she waiting for her younger sister, our Aunty Ann? It wouldn't be easy telling Mum that Aunty Ann had passed away. We had initially wanted Mum to get better, planning we would tell her once she was out of hospital. As this was not to be, we now felt we had to tell her. We knew she had heard as she grunted.

My brother chose to spend the night with Mum, my niece went home and my sister and I left to go to the B&B. I was grateful for my own room, to have my own space and offload through tears the stress and emotions of the day. I pulled the duvet over my head so my sister could not hear me crying in the next room, although I'm sure she was crying too. I had faith in the God Mum had once taught me about. I had always continued to rely on Him when I needed Him, and also to say thank you for good things in life. Tonight, I asked Him to take my mother and relieve her pain. 'Why are you putting her through this?' I cried into the pillow. I had a disturbed night and each time I awoke I pleaded again with God to take my mother.

Chapter 13

Hospital hell

As we walked down to breakfast I asked my sister if we could eat somewhere different this morning. Without questioning why, when we had paid for breakfast upfront, she asked, 'Where do you want to go?'

'Anywhere. Let's find a café.'

That's what we did. We ordered a cooked breakfast and two mugs of tea. We didn't talk much; we had our own thoughts racing through our heads.

As we walked onto the ward we acknowledged the nurses as we passed them, and greeted our mother and brother as we entered her room. Keith was sitting in the big recliner chair next to Mum so Ann and I sat on the two chairs on the other side. We were all looking strained from lack of sleep. My brother told us that Mum hadn't woken yet this morning and that Vic would be in later.

I cleaned my mother's eyes with a tissue and found a nurse to ask for something to moisten her lips. This should have been in her care plan, but staff were not doing it regularly.

Our conversation was ad hoc between silences and checking for messages on the mobile phones which we had silenced so as not to disturb Mum.

Vic knocked on the door. (No one else bothered.) My brother went for a sleep in his campervan in the hospital car park and Vic sat in his chair. Both my sister and I had offered him our rooms to sleep and shower, but he wanted to stay close to Mum, 'Just in case…'

We checked what time the morphine driver would need changing and my sister alerted the nurses to the fact that this would be within one hour.

I stood leaning against the bed rails and my eyes followed the 'gurgling' sound coming from the new VAC dressing machine. For the first time it seemed to be working and draining fluids well from Mum's body.

'Look!' I said pointing to the tube. 'I hadn't noticed this before. Had you?'

'No, I hadn't,' my niece replied.

'Nor me,' added my sister as she came back in.

'I wonder if the previous machine was actually working. If it was, Mum's pressure sore should have got better instead of worse.'

As usual, staff came in to Mum's room without knocking. Fortunately the staff nurse was friendlier that day.

Two staff nurses came in to change the morphine driver. As it was an easy procedure and would not cause any indignity to Mum, we stayed in the room, standing against the wall to allow room for the nurses to do their job. I looked at my watch; it was 4.15 pm.

'Thank you,' I said to myself, in relief that Mum would have the morphine to keep her free from pain.

'It needs two qualified staff to do this; it's a controlled drug and one has to check it and the other one administers it,' one of the nurses told us.

'I know,' I thought to myself, 'I've just written a workbook on the subject – *Safe Handling and Administration of Medication.*'

My niece, who was also in the health profession, and I looked at each other and then at the staff nurses, smiled at them and thanked them as they finished and left the room. I looked at the signatures on the morphine driver and made a note of them, determined that Mum would not suffer as she had yesterday.

We fell back into our routine of laughing, eating and chatting. Mum gave an occasional grunt and we knew she could hear us. She could hear us being happy and hopefully when she did pass away she would have these memories to take with her.

My niece had a new iPhone. She played *Red* by Daniel Merriweather at my request. We knew the words – 'I can't do this by myself… my time on the outside is over…' would always remind us of this time.

At 9 pm Mum became distressed and was vocalising again. On checking the morphine driver, my niece noticed that the arm of the driver wasn't locked around the end of the syringe. Mum had gone without morphine for over four hours. The staff nurse checked the driver and admitted it was inserted incorrectly. She took it out and left the room. Another staff nurse came in, inserted the morphine into the driver and said she was waiting for the doctor to authorise a 'top-up', which he did. The doctor visited and apologised for what had happened; he was deeply embarrassed. He had told us that Mum would be treated with dignity and respect as she went along the Liverpool Care Pathway. There had been little sign of that thus far.

I told the doctor that I had really had enough of this poor treatment. He apologised again and as he left the room he touched my Mum's lower leg, as a way of an apology.

We watched Mum and waited for her to be calm again. We drifted in and out of conversation. Mum was lying with her eyes closed and didn't say anything; this was Okay; the morphine was working.

Much later Vic, Ann and I left the ward. Vic went home and Ann and I drove to the B&B. I went for a walk alone along the seafront. Again, in desperation and in tears, I asked God to take Mum.

'Dear God, my mum is a beautiful, lovely and kind lady. It's heartbreaking to see her let down like this by the NHS. Not one ward, but two. TWO wards have not treated her properly. How long are you going to let this go on for? You are in charge now, God, and therefore responsible for what happens to my mum. I'm sorry to have a go at you, God, but I am *so* angry… upset…, mourning the loss of my aunt and now my mum… Please take her,' I begged. 'Don't hurt her anymore. Amen.'

I tossed and turned in bed, knowing there was no point in getting up as there was nothing to do and nowhere to go. I lay motionless. I looked at the clock: 2.30 am. I gave a big sigh, leant over and put the light on before getting up and reaching for my note pad. I started scribbling down what had happened and the tears started. They landed on my pad and smudged some of the writing, but I couldn't stop them and I didn't care anyway. Finally, I threw the pad and pen down and the pen bounced off the bed. I drew my knees up to my chest and cried some more. Through my crying I pleaded again to God to take my mother.

Chapter 14

Peace at last for Mum

I went for a walk along the seafront before breakfast. It was too early for any pedestrians to be about, apart from one or two joggers, which I was grateful for as I didn't want to engage in conversation. I crossed the road at the traffic lights and ahead of me was a man sitting on the grass with an empty bottle of beer beside him. I attempted to walk straight past him and kept looking straight ahead.

'Go on, put a smile on yer face, luv,' he told me. I did force a smile at him and walked away. 'If only he knew,' I thought to myself. I walked along the seafront recalling lovely memories of years gone by.

'You're going to find me a new home… You're going to find me a new home…' kept coming into my head and I tried my best to dismiss it. I was convinced I had let Mum down; I hadn't found her a new home. If only a social worker had been in place when Mum was fit for discharge…

Ann and I were eating breakfast with the older guests when her mobile rang and I watched her face for a reaction.

'We've got to go,' she said and within seconds we were running out of the B&B and driving to the hospital. We ran from the car park into reception and up two flights of stairs, passing a doctor on the way who said, 'Someone's in a rush. Has anyone died?' Huffing and puffing, we stopped for a second or two to get our breath before going up the remaining stairs. We ran into the ward and into Mum's room. My sister in front went to hug Mum and I stayed just inside the door looking at my brother and the nurse who was also in the room. The nurse told us that the doctor needed to visit and she left the room. We hugged Mum and each other. At 8.45 am, Mum had passed away. Peace at last – for her.

The NHS website, in the pages devoted to 'end of life', includes this statement: 'The care of the deceased and their relatives should always be carried out with respect, dignity and empathy, and in accordance with the local policy.' I do not know what most people experience, but we didn't receive any 'after care'. The nurse came back in to say the doctor was on his way. She was very cold and distant, and showed no compassion. Was she new to dealing with loss, I wondered?

When the doctor arrived, we left the room and went into the corridor. The nicest thing that had happened during all this was when a member of staff, who remembered how we all liked our tea, brought us out a tray of drinks. I wanted to hug her. We sat in the corridor outside the ward, crying.

My sister asked who wanted to go to see Mum and say their last goodbyes. I didn't as I felt I had said mine already; Ann said that she wanted to go in and did so. I went up the corridor to the toilet and was taken aback at how my anger grew with every step. I put up the hood of my top and marched to the toilet. I sat on it and cried. I washed my face with cold water and looked in the mirror to find that I was a 'hoodie'. I realised how comforting it was to have something surrounding my head which enabled me to block out everyone and everything.

On the way back into the ward I stopped by the Ward Sister's office to express my concerns about all the poor care my mother had experienced since being on this ward. Although I would be putting everything in writing, I wanted to tell her there and then because I did not want anyone else going through what Mum and we, as her family, had just experienced. She gave me a photocopy of the complaints procedure and I refused it. My mother deserved more than that flimsy piece of paper and I would be writing to the Chief Executive.

I joined my family in the side room – Mum's room, our family room. I picked up the bottle of perfume I had bought Mum and held it close to me.

'Spray the perfume once more,' my sister said and through my tears I did so.

Numb with grief, we went to the canteen and had a drink. We didn't talk much. We hugged and told each other that Mum was out of pain now. We had to be positive for her.

The death certificate said the cause of death was 'septicaemia and pneumonia'. Mum had been admitted to hospital with fractures to the tibia and femur. These fractures were not the cause of her death. She died from blood poisoning.

I googled the NHS website for clarification of what these conditions were and found that Mum had had some of the symptoms. Of course, we had not known what to look out for. I learned that 'sepsis' is life-threatening in that an infection causes the body's immune system to go into overdrive that, if not treated successfully, will lead to septic shock and the failure of all the body's key organs. I gleaned that the number of cases had been rising and there had been over 30,000 incidents in the UK the previous year. (www.nhs.uk/conditions/Blood-poisoning/Pages/Introduction.aspx)

The symptoms of septicaemia that we were aware Mum had had included 'confusion or disorientation' and 'nausea and vomiting'. As she became increasingly ill, we did not know what the symptoms indicated, but trained staff should have picked up the implications as a matter of course. Perhaps they had and just not told us?

I had been aware pneumonia was a risk for anybody who was bedbound. This was why I had remonstrated with staff when they had made Mum lie flat. Googling this condition I learned that the lungs become inflamed owing to infection and the tiny air sacs where oxygen exchange occurs become filled with fluid. It is essentially like drowning! The NHS website said anybody could get pneumonia and up to 11 adults in 1000 in the UK are affected each year. The people who are most vulnerable, not unexpectedly, are the very young and the very old, people who smoke and people who have other health conditions or weakened immune systems: www.nhs.uk/conditions/pneumonia/pages/introduction.aspx

The pneumonia symptoms that Mum had had included 'feeling generally unwell; sweating and shivering; loss of appetite; pain in the chest'. So were all those tests for the pain in Mum's chest completely off the point? And why had nobody told us?

. . . .

If someone you care for has died in hospital and you have concerns you want to raise about their care:

- You don't need to do so immediately. Give yourself a breathing space.
- To make a complaint you will need the patient's notes. The next of kin has a right to receive these. If you are not the next of kin you will need to inform the medical records office and they will send you out a form for the next of kin to complete, giving permission for you to apply to receive these records, so request them as soon as you can. To do so you need to contact the Medical Records Department at the hospital.
- There is no time limit on your part to contact the office and request the records. However, there is a time limit that the hospital has to adhere to. For example, at my local hospital, if I or a relative had been in the hospital in the past 21 days the hospital would need to respond within x weeks. Outside of these 21 days they have 40 days to respond.

Chapter 15

Saying good-bye

So soon after Aunty Ann's, we had to start thinking about another funeral: our mother's. My brother made the arrangements and my sister and I put together something about Mum for the priest to read out. As we did this we cried, but rarely at the same time. There were many pauses with neither of us speaking. Once, my sister broke the silence. 'Come on, let's get this done,' and we both started talking about what we would like in the piece. Our conversation changed direction many times from talking about the funeral to the way Mum had been treated in hospital and the injuries she had sustained in the nursing home.

My brother found a lovely and very fitting verse, which he would read out. He had invited some staff from the nursing home. I didn't know if these were the people who had caused Mum's injuries. I was not happy about them being invited, but they might have been really good staff and nothing to do with the injuries.

I got photographs of Mum and Aunty Ann enlarged, put them into frames and took them to the funeral. The two sisters would be together again. I cancelled my train tickets for work the following week and again wrote on the form the reason was 'bereavement', as I had done some weeks before for Aunty Ann's funeral.

I awoke early with a wet pillow; I had been crying in my sleep.

I had seen Mum smiling, saying, 'You're going to find me a new home. You're going to find me a new home.' 'You were so happy then, Mum,' I thought, 'and I am really sorry that I couldn't get you a new home.' I turned over onto the other pillow and cried into that.

There was a lot of talking and texting about who would go in whose car down to the west coast and who wanted to stay in a B&B and who wanted to drive down and back in the one day. The drivers for the trip questioned the easiest way to go down. To be honest I didn't care about the best route. We just needed to get there safely. Another funeral. We hadn't been able to mourn Aunty Ann yet; I so hoped it would all be over soon and we would be able to mourn both sisters together.

I managed to fit those who wanted to stay overnight into B&Bs, not all at the same one but at least we would all be there on the day. I managed to get the last vacant room in my usual B&B and I was delighted to be staying there. It had been a home from home to me for many weeks.

A convoy of us drove from east to west coasts the day before the funeral; we kept in touch by text on the journey. We met at the service stations. We didn't talk much, having nothing to say. 'Let's just get through today,' I told myself.

We went to the funeral home to see Mum's body. I stared at her in the coffin as I had stared at Aunty Ann in hers six weeks earlier. I knew I was staring but I couldn't help it. I stared because I was numb and I couldn't move.

On the day the sun shone and when we had all arrived it was like déjà vu, but in a different venue and in a different part of England. Same family, wearing similar clothes to those we had just six weeks before. We hugged without speaking; facial expressions said everything.

We waited for Mum's coffin to arrive and whilst doing so had a group photo taken.

At Aunty Ann's funeral we had all been seated before they brought the coffin in. At Mum's funeral we were asked to wait and follow the coffin in. The funeral was lovely, if you can call any funeral 'lovely'. I laid the enlarged framed photos of Mum and Aunty Ann side by side by the coffin. I listened hard to the words being said. I began to understand that it was now time for Mum to leave us. People began to cry, softly for a while and then more vocally.

The Manager and two members of staff from the nursing home came. The Manager tried to make eye contact with me, but I avoided it. I didn't want her there. I didn't know exactly how the injuries had occurred as there had been different stories, none of them verifiable, but in the end the Manager has overall responsibility for everyone and everything that happens in a home.

We went to a pub for the wake and toasted Mum and Aunty Ann. It was a glorious, sunny June evening; some of us went for a walk and some of us lay on the beach. The sun was still hot at 9 pm.

That night I was shattered and went to bed thinking I would be able to sleep, but I found I couldn't. My night was interrupted several times by reliving Mum shouting and screaming when the nurses put her on her back with the catheter pipe pressing into the grade 4 pressure sore. After getting back to sleep for the fourth or fifth time, I then relived Mum crying for us to do something when the morphine had run out and then again when the staff nurses had not set up the morphine driver properly… I lay in bed asking myself yet again how this could have happened.

I managed to get back to sleep again and I dreamt. I was holding Mum's hand as I sat by her bed and slowly and softly her hand was loosening its grip and then there was nothing, all blank. And then I was standing, leaning against the wall, watching one of the ducks. The duck left the ground and my eyes followed it as it spread its wings and gained height. It slowly turned into an angel and flew softly higher and higher. The angel looked happy and it turned its head to me and nodded before flying up, up into the clouds until I could see it no more. Bye Mum, love you xx.

I awoke in the morning and recalled this dream and my crying was soothed by feeling sure that Mum's spirit had risen and flown away.

Spreading Mum's ashes added to the feeling of peace. The sun was shining as we walked through the trees and we found a nice sunny spot to spread the ashes. A man from the cremation company read a beautiful poem about finding peace. Some ash fell on his shiny, polished black shoes and it took a tinge of sadness away for a few seconds.

One at Rest
(Author unknown)

Think of me as one at rest,
for me you should not weep.
I have no pain, no troubled thoughts
for I am just asleep.
The living thinking me that was,
is now forever still
And life goes on without me now,
as time forever will.

If your heart is heavy now
because I've gone away,
Dwell not long upon it, friend,
For none of us can stay.
Those of you who liked me,
I sincerely thank you all
And those of you who loved me,
I thank you most of all.

And in my fleeting lifespan,
as time went rushing by,
I found some time to hesitate,
to laugh, to love, to cry.
Matters it now if time began
If time will ever cease?
I was here, I used it all,
and now I am at peace.

'And you are at peace, Mum,' I thought. 'You are with Aunty Ann and I hope you are together up there looking after each other like sisters should.'

My sister and I said, 'We've lost the adults.' We were the adults now; we'd taken their place. And there was work to be done.

Chapter 16

My mission to promote better care begins

Not all care services and nursing homes have a training budget or, if they do, it may be very limited. In an attempt to raise standards in older people's services I offered some free training on 'Dignity in Care' and 'Care Quality Commission Essential Standards on Quality and Safety requirements'. Both courses were snapped up quickly by some services. I wished I could have offered more.

Every morning waking up was as painful as the previous mornings had been, especially when I searched my brain to see what I was doing that day. I cried. I felt raw, still suffering after the loss of Mum and Aunty Ann.

That day I was delivering a training session on Dignity in Care to staff who supported older people. I had a large group of 20. Usually I teach up to 14, but I guessed that as it was a free course, the manager had put in as many as she could.

The staff came from a variety of cultures and were very knowledgeable. They shared their knowledge on which cultures liked different foods and liked to be washed/bathed differently and those who needed support to have prayer time.

I was pleasantly surprised when two staff members shared their stories on how and why they had had to report staff who had abused some individuals they were supposed to supporting. They kept the details confidential and did not give any names of the individuals who had been abused or staff involved, but it was clear that some staff had been suspended on full pay whilst investigations had taken place.

I had the utmost respect for these two people for reporting their concerns. It couldn't have been easy with the individuals concerned being part of their team, but they had done it for the welfare of the people they were looking after. These two staff wanted and needed to talk about it and I gave them the opportunity in the break times to do this on a one-to-one basis with me. Before they started talking I told them that I was bound by confidentiality but also duty of care and would have to report anything I had concerns about. Confidentiality has to be breached if a vulnerable person is at risk of abuse or harm.

Back in the training session, the staff members were very much aware of their 'duty of care'. They understood that all professionals have a duty of care to the people they support and that they needed to ensure that the individuals they supported did not suffer any unreasonable harm or loss. Some, however, found the issue of choice difficult to work with and understand. Many people, whether they have a learning disability, or are older, or have dementia, may need support to make informed choices, and this includes informed choices about risks. People receiving care must not be overprotected and withdrawn from life. They must be supported and, with the aid of a risk assessment, enabled to fulfil their dreams, needs and wishes.

On my 'Dignity in Care' course I wouldn't usually cover manual handling and hoisting, but since my late mother's 'accident' with the hoist, I had been asking questions about hoisting at every opportunity I got. I asked about the law, the Health and Safety Act 1974 and, in particular, the Manual Handling Operations Regulations 1992. These are regulations that staff need to adhere to. Each individual requiring manual handling should be risk assessed and it will be stated on the risk assessment and in the individual's care plan how s/he is to be moved, what equipment should be used and how many staff should be involved in the manoeuvre.

All was going well until I asked this question: 'Do you always use two staff if it says two staff?' Many said 'Yes', but one staff member said, 'No, not always.'

I could feel anger brewing up inside and I wasn't sure if it was because of her blasé attitude or because of what had happened to Mum. (Probably both!) I pointed out the dangers, but she responded, 'I've done it loads of times and no one's been hurt.' I finished this subject by reiterating what they should do and informed the Manager during the tea break that this member of staff needed to understand what was meant by safe practice and why it mattered.

Chapter 17

Tackling the hospital

I drafted a letter to the Chief Executive of the hospital. I could not bring myself to do it for some months and it took me a long time as I had so much to write about. I left my first draft for a few days more and, after altering it slightly, I sealed the envelope and posted it. It was November when I walked to the post box, and carried on walking, glad that I had not seen anyone I knew. I began to think about something I had heard on the news that morning about an older lady who had been found dead in her house. She had been dead for some weeks. In times gone by, many people had their milk delivered; the milkman knew their movements and if there were problems he would alert someone. The milkman and the postman, or woman, could be the only individuals some older people saw each day.

I felt relieved that I had started the ball rolling as far as the hospital was concerned. I had, of course, started challenging Social Services and the Care Quality Commission in the early days after Mum's double accident, but had become too exhausted and busy trying to make sure Mum was okay in the hospital. I had had no energy to continue that fight at the time. I knew then that things were wrong; when I had had a bit of time to think more clearly I realised I had to challenge all these organisations. But the system required me to tackle each one separately. It was very hard to have to make all the running, and to do so in the face of their overwhelming indifference.

The hospital did not respond to my November letter. Six months on I wrote again. This was hard as each piece of correspondence I had to write or read caused me to relive what had happened to Mum; it left me feeling shattered and tearful, but it was something I had to do. Now I wanted a reply; I needed a reply; we as a family needed a reply.

I received two white envelopes on the same day with the hospital stamp on each. The first envelope had my name and address on it, but the letter was addressed to a man and the letter was 'with reference to your late wife…'. As I read on, the hospital thanked him for informing them about his concerns and said they would look into them. I opened the second envelope and the letter inside was addressed to me: it thanked me for informing them about my concerns and said that they would look into them. I wondered how many letters of complaint the hospital received each day.

Although I was really shocked to have received a private and confidential letter which was wrongly addressed, I judged that at this stage it did not warrant my 'causing a scene' as it would take away the emphasis from my much more fundamental complaint. Instead I just put it in the envelope with my next letter to the hospital.

After another few weeks, the hospital wrote again, responding to some (but not all) of my itemised concerns. Firstly, they had this to say about my criticisms of nursing records: 'You rightly make several observations regarding our documentation. The Trust has recognised this and is currently in the process of introducing new nursing documentation that will promote clearer and more robust record keeping.' That was something.

On the subject of my mother's pressure sore, they said: 'We apologise for failing to inform you of the outcome of the investigation into your mother's hospital-acquired pressure ulcer. At that time it became apparent we had several patients who had developed pressure ulcers. As a result of this we undertook an external review which highlighted several problems with the way in which we managed pressure ulcers. This review was completed in August and we have now taken several steps to reduce the likelihood of such ulcers developing.' That also sounded like a positive, if they really were going to take these steps.

I had also mentioned my concerns about confusion between the Bereavement Office and the Patient Advice Liaison Service (PALS) office: 'Volunteers on reception will be reminded to ensure they direct people appropriately. Action by the PALS Manager.' I very much hoped this would be done.

I had said how troubled we had been that we had been given no information about the Liverpool Care Pathway: 'Bereavement staff to be reminded to ensure appropriate involvement of the Palliative Care Team.'

On the attitude of the student nurse: 'Mentors to discuss with students. Action by Ward Sisters / Clinical Educator.' Hmm. And on the attitude of staff generally: 'Staff to be appraised of the impact of their behaviour. The complaint is to be shared with all ward staff concerned in a facilitated discussion, learning to be identified. Action by Ward Sisters.' Hmm, again.

I felt unconvinced. The hospital had written an action plan but there was no proof the actions would be carried out. I had no faith in them. I searched the internet for help. After a lot of searching, I read about the Parliamentary and Health Services Ombudsman. I learned that the role of the Ombudsman's office is to consider complaints that the NHS in England (and other bodies) has not acted properly or fairly or has provided a poor service. 'We work to put things right where we can and to share lessons learned to improve public services,' their website said (www.ombudsman.org.uk/).

I rang the Ombudsman's office and told them what had happened. I was advised to 'Write a letter to the hospital and if you get no response come back to us.'

'Can't you do anything now?' I pleaded. I wanted them to step in and investigate what had happened, and why. As I had no trust in the hospital, given that *two* wards had let my mother down, I wanted an outsider with some clout to intervene.

'Keep writing until they do not respond. Then we can help you.' So I wrote back to the hospital. In response, this time I received a telephone call from the Complaints Manager saying that the Director of Nursing (the same Director I and my sister had met with while Mum was still alive) had asked if we wanted to meet with him and the two Ward Sisters who had been in charge of the two wards Mum had been on, if this could be arranged. This would be to discuss the points in my letter. She said that the Ward Sisters would be better able to explain face to face what had been put in place rather than describing this in a letter. She also apologised for not answering all my concerns in the first place. I said I would discuss the hospital's invitation with my brother and sister and get back to her.

We agreed that we needed time to think about it. If we went to the hospital, would we just say our piece, listen to what they said, shake hands, and then leave things there? We talked about all the issues that had not been addressed satisfactorily in the hospital's letter, especially the occasion when the healthcare assistant had elbowed me out of the way and force-fed Mum, leaving her retching; the letter from the hospital had described this as 'a misunderstanding'. If the letter meant that this had been addressed, then that would be something, but saying it was 'a misunderstanding' did not fit well with taking any action and could imply that their standards were just appallingly low. However, if we did not accept the offered meeting, we could not see what else we might achieve by other means. Overall, it was worth a try. I rang our usual B&B and booked rooms for the following week.

About the same time as this, I also received an email from one of the local councils for which I do regular work, asking if I would take the lead in an investigation of alleged bad practice. I needed time to think about how I should respond to this request. My nerves were too raw; I was not feeling 100 per cent mentally stable in the aftermath of Mum's death. Could I cope with such an investigation, or conduct it impartially, when I was in the middle of something similar on my own behalf?

Facing this traumatic situation, I received this text from a friend who is also in the care sector: 'I admire u greatly 4 ur determination, commitment and patience. 4 wot it is worth I also admire the approach ur takin.' He will never know how much this message helped to keep me going.

Chapter 18

Anniversaries

I was laughing with my mum, talking about getting her another home and asking what she would like in her room there in the way of furniture and décor. We decided that I would give up my career, buy a bungalow for Mum and me, and we would get some staff to help with the care. We were both laughing and enjoying being together… We had found the bungalow we wanted and were about to move in… Then I woke up and realised it was a dream. Throughout the day it gave me an image of Mum laughing and it made me happy.

We were going through the first anniversaries of my Aunty Ann's and my mum's birthdays and deaths, and Mother's Day as well. A painful tunnel to be in. I knew we would all get through it and it would become easier over time, but at that moment it was very painful. I planted a tree in the back garden; the flowers are first yellow and then orange.

Looking back now, I realise I was suffering badly from stress and delayed shock. I had developed what I was eventually told by a specialist was 'idiopathic tinnitus' (ringing in the ears without an identifiable cause) brought on by the stress of what had happened to Mum. I had known there was a link as the ringing in my ears had started while I was staying on the ward to look after her. It was sometimes so bad it would wake me up at night. It was like the sound of a kettle whistling right there in the bedroom.

I recorded in my diary:

Entry 1: Mum passed away a year ago tomorrow. I went to the supermarket today to buy some doughnuts… comfort eating. I am hoping that after tomorrow my stress levels will reduce and the ringing in my ears will stop.

Entry 2: We had a lovely family meal last night and raised our glasses to Mum and Aunty Ann. I went to bed, totally relaxed, but within a short time my body started to shake. I was unable to control my limbs. My body went cold and I curled up into the fetal position to try and keep warm. I knew I didn't feel right so I slowly got up and held onto the bed and then onto the door to get another quilt from the airing cupboard. I walked slowly and held onto the bed as much as I could. I threw the quilt over it and got back into bed. My body continued to shake and the shaking got faster and my body was uncontrollable. I thought about the phone but I was shaking too much and could not control my hand to pick it up. The whole of my body was shaking too much…

I fell asleep sometime after 3 am and when I awoke this morning I was still in the fetal position but my hands were clasped together to the left of my head. The same position Mum was in when she was crying and holding onto the bed rails in the hospital. I must have delayed shock.

Entry 3: I awoke before the alarm went off and, unusually these days, got out of bed. As this morning went on I realised that I was a little happy, I had a little sunshine in my heart. It is one year and two days since Mum passed away and today has been the first time that I have felt a little happiness. Not a lot, but a little and, believe me, it feels so good. I hope that this happiness will continue to grow.

• •

Three useful websites to help with bereavement are:

http://dying.about.com/od/thegrievingprocess/a/grief-process.htm (Grief and Mourning: what's normal and what's not?)

http://www.cruse.org.uk/

http://www.bereavementuk.co.uk/

Chapter 19

Tackling the hospital – continued

I awoke to the alarm going off and wondered why I had to get up at this hour on a Sunday. Then I remembered I had to prepare for the long car journey with my sister. For a few seconds my mind told me we would be going to see Mum. Then, as I grew wider awake it dawned on me that we would not be seeing Mum and that we were going to the west coast for a meeting to discuss why the nurses and doctors had treated her in the way they had.

The next day, at 11.30 am, Keith, Ann and I went into a meeting room... and the fire alarm went off. There was a bit of discussion about whether it was a fire drill, but I said, 'It's been going on too long. Let's get out,' and led the meeting outside. When it was safe to go back in, we sat at the table in the meeting room and introductions were made. The meeting consisted of the Director of Nursing, the Complaints Manager, the Ward Sister responsible for the ward Mum had passed away on, my brother, sister and me. I led the meeting and time and time again the word 'Sorry' was heard but it was too late for it to provide any satisfaction or sense of closure.

When it came to the healthcare assistant who had elbowed me in the stomach and shovelled food into my mother's mouth, leaving her retching, they said they did not condone force-feeding and the incident would be treated seriously, possibly as a Safeguarding issue, and appropriate disciplinary action would be taken. I explained I was myself a Safeguarding trainer and what I had seen her do constituted abuse. They assured us they were now employing a Safeguarding Manager for one and a half days a week and that they would be rolling out a Safeguarding programme; the healthcare assistant would be put on this if she had not already received this training.

I asked why no one had intervened at the time. The Ward Sister, quite bravely I thought, said: 'My staff were too embarrassed to do so as so many things were going wrong. On reflection, I should have done something.'

The Director of Nursing refused to put anything on the personnel records of staff who had given poor care, because 'the staff have rights', despite the fact that little concern had been shown for my mother's rights. It was painful listening.

We had been assured that our queries would be answered in this meeting but it still felt as though the importance of what we were saying was being ignored. Of course more training was worthwhile for all concerned, but we did not feel confident that anything had fundamentally changed. When the minutes of the meeting came, they also contradicted what had been said on the day about the healthcare assistant – there was no mention of Safeguarding. To quote from the minutes

Pressure ulcer: *Action taken by the Trust in relation to pressure ulcers – training to address the gap in skills and knowledge on the use of equipment; Trust Tissue Viability Team's remit redefined and strengthened.*
Syringe driver: *Staff identified have completed additional training. Apologies offered in relation to the incident that occurred.*
Liverpool Pathway: *Agreed that this is a planned pathway of*

care; pain management should have been included in the plan; acknowledged this fundamental care was apparently not managed effectively. It has also been recognised through the National Patient Survey results that the Trust can improve in this area. This will be addressed. Unregistered staff have been reminded they are patient advocates and should document observations or conversations with patients, especially in relation to pain, and specify who they pass messages onto in order to strengthen accountability.

Nutrition*: Designated roles are now identified for staff on the ward at meal times.*

Communication*: Recognised that communication was at times poor and apologies were offered.*

Catheter*: It is unacceptable that this incident occurred. Staff attitude is being addressed by the Sister to ensure that improvements are made and a similar incident does not happen in the future.*

Co-ordinating care when things are not going well*: '(....) ward sister accepted that she should have been more proactive and has learnt from this experience. In future she will take on this lead role.*

Nursing auxiliary's inappropriate behaviour*: The Ward Sister immediately met with the nursing auxiliary [that is, the healthcare assistant] and explained that you had thought she elbowed you out of the way and shovelled food into your mother's mouth. The nursing auxiliary was distraught and upset at the suggestion and stated that she was responding to the fact that your mother's nutritional intake had been highlighted as a cause of concern. The Ward Sister believes that raising the nursing auxiliary's awareness of how her behaviour was perceived was sufficient to deal with the situation.*

Nursing student's inappropriate behaviour*: As a result of your concerns, the dignity and privacy of patients was highlighted as part of (...) student nurse's learning plan and*

addressed in his on-going clinical training. This plan will be
assessed as part of his clinical competence.

We also needed to know why Mum had died and wondered if we would learn more by seeing her medical records. At the end of the meeting I asked for a copy of these and was surprised that this request was accepted without demur. Within a few weeks I received the records. There were so many different forms that the hospital staff had been expected to complete. Some had not been completed fully. Was that due to lack of time or disorganisation? I wondered. There were two copies of the Liverpool Care Pathway care plan to help Mum die with no pain and with dignity. I wondered why there were two plans and not just one, and whether, if one of these had been completed fully, Mum's last few days would have been better. I would never know.

We wanted to know why the staff had not treated Mum well, and why, when she had been admitted for two fractures, she had died of something unrelated. Only when the hospital acknowledged these 'whys' could they really take action to stop anything like this happening again. I shared my family's disappointment with the meeting in a letter to the Chief Executive. We had been assured that the Director of Nursing would answer our outstanding queries, but he had not. He had addressed the detail, not the big questions. Furthermore, we did not agree with his saying that he could not record anything on the staff's personnel files 'because they had rights'. I added that overall we had no faith in the management of the hospital. I waited for a reply to arrive.

August came and no letter had arrived in response. I kept assuming it would come the following day. Then there was a voice message on my mobile from the Complaints Manager at the hospital. She apologised for the delay in sending a reply to me, but said this was because the Chief Executive was not happy with the contents of the letter they had drafted and she wanted it amended.

I had told myself and my family that once we got this letter from the Chief Executive I would challenge the hospital no longer. I was very tired and pursuing these issues continued to consume my waking and sleeping life. By now it was over two years since my mother had died. I could at least feel some achievement in getting many things changed at the hospital – for example, re-styled patient records to include important information, such as, how patients wish to communicate verbally and non-verbally, their likes and dislikes, and what they liked to be called.

When we finally received the promised letter, its last paragraph read: 'Finally, may I take this opportunity to say how very sorry we are that we failed to provide the level of care due to your mother and your family and the distress that this caused at such a very difficult time. It is my hope that this letter has gone some way to assure you of our commitment to continually learn and improve the quality of care for our patients.'

'At least now you can have closure,' my friends told me, taking this letter at face value. But I couldn't. I had no faith in the hospital actually doing the things they had said, nor in these small changes really making a difference. The same people were still in charge and nobody was calling them to account. I could not have closure until all of those who had let my mother and my family down had admitted fault and given me assurance that what we had been through would not happen again to others.

The letter did not give us closure for another reason. The contents did not flow and it read as though some areas had been copied and pasted in the wrong places; it included responses to things that I had not written about in my last letter. This made me realise that I was not going to get any further by corresponding with the hospital. They were not going to tell me anything more. Now was the time for me to make a formal claim.

Chapter 20

Solicitors

You may be wondering why I did not seek the help of a solicitor. In fact I did just that a few months after my mother's death. I looked locally and went to see one of them. I was fragile and I had to swallow hard before telling my story, but as I started to tell it I was interrupted: 'Now, dear, older people do die. How old was your mum?'

I opened my mouth with shock. I swallowed before croaking, 'Seventy-eight'. And for the first time he looked up from his folder and saw I was about to cry. I fought back the tears.

'I'm sorry, dear. It wasn't meant to come out that way, but many old people go into hospital and die.' He couldn't help me and advised that I needed a solicitor who dealt with medical or clinical negligence.

There were numerous solicitors on the internet but I wanted one locally who I could see and sit with and explain what had happened and what we wanted as a family, which was to find out what could be done about the staff who had caused so much pain and harm to Mum and the rest of us. After numerous telephone calls I found there were none locally with the necessary specialisation. Eventually I found two in the City and rang both. The PAs took my details and said that they would ring me back if they could help.

One solicitor rang me that evening and offered me an hour

instead of the usual half-hour free consultation. (The other rang back two weeks later and I had to decline.) We set a date to meet at his office. I went and told him everything. He listened carefully and said he felt there was a case but couldn't confirm this until he had seen the accident forms and correspondence from the hospital. He was very patient with me and asked many questions. He explained that once he was involved, all correspondence between the hospital and me would have to stop and he would then concentrate on the key issue from the point of view of medical negligence – the grade 4 pressure sore.

We decided that I needed to complete my own investigation into why the staff had treated Mum so badly, so he patiently waited for the hospital to finish answering the questions in my letters before he started looking into the case thoroughly.

There was also the question of how we would pay for the solicitor's help. He asked me to check my house insurance as many house insurances covered legal claims. Unfortunately, I did not have this cover and it was too late to change my insurers as I had started the (informal) proceedings already by communicating with the hospital. The solicitor and I corresponded via email mostly and when I received Mum's hospital records I took them to him. However, we still had to wait for the accident form and papers from the nursing home and this took two whole years.

Two years after my mother's death in June 2009, I finally received her records from the nursing home. An entry in the daily records stated, 'Sling is too small, please risk assess'. There were two accident reports, one written by the Manager and one written by one of the staff who had actually been using the hoist when the accident occurred. There were also two CQC regulation 37 reports (a form that managers use to inform the Care Quality Commission of accidents and incidents). In addition, there was some scribble on the back of the Manager's timesheet saying,

'This should not have happened. Ask Keith [my brother] for his response'. I felt sick.

I put all the information together and saw conflicting views as to what had taken place. The accident forms said that the accident had happened whilst Mum was being transferred to the bed, but the actual account was that it had happened as she was being adjusted in her chair, having been hoisted there from her bed.

I could not understand how Mum could have suffered fractures to both legs simply by sliding, falling and catching one leg underneath the wheelchair as she slipped. Mum had not been able to stand up or bear weight on her legs for many years and the accident forms suggested that the staff had tried to stand her up.

Now that we had all the documentation together we discussed as a family whether we wanted to go ahead with the solicitor. We knew it would be very stressful and potentially far more expensive than any of us could afford. We also knew that the solicitor would only deal with the pressure sore, and not all the other issues we wanted addressed. At the same time, I realised I was not being fair on myself trying to find out from four different agencies what had happened to Mum and why. I met with my sister and told her I had to bow out of co-ordinating the case. It was too much. I explained to the solicitor that I could not go on and Mum's records were returned to us. I felt a sense of relief, but it could not last.

· ·

What you may need to know about involving a solicitor
- Before you contact a solicitor, write down what you want to achieve by doing so; this will help you in talking to the solicitor, but also in determining if involving a solicitor is appropriate.

- There is a limited number of solicitors who can be registered to represent claims for medical negligence.
- Make sure you get a full picture of the likely costs that involving a solicitor will incur.
- Ensure you have 'legal' cover on your house insurance before making any contact with the party (organisation or individual) against which you want to take action.
- Most solicitors offer a free exploratory meeting before deciding to take a case. The discussion involved can help you decide what it is you want to achieve.
- Be aware that most cases of medical negligence are settled out of court; this means the 'victim' receives some compensatory payment but without the party being sued, admitting fault or saying sorry.

Chapter 21

Tackling the Safeguarding Team and the Care Quality Commission – again

My mother's story was so complicated. She had been the victim of poor care in both her nursing home and the hospital, which meant having to tackle the various agencies involved separately, but at the same time.

We were still waiting for the Safeguarding Team Leader to get back to us to follow up the concerns I had raised about the nursing home right at the start. Now I no longer had to be with Mum in the hospital I could take these concerns up again. I rang the Team Leader's office and left a message for her to ring me. I did not hear anything. Eleven days later I rang her office again and was told she was off sick. She should be back at work on Thursday, they said. Three days later I rang to find she was out of the office and would not be back for six days. Ten days later I rang again. She was in supervision, I was told. On each occasion I left a message for her to ring me.

I was wondering what I could possibly do to get an answer, when the very next day she left a message on my mobile at 1.30 pm. She then rang me later that day and explained that she had sent numerous emails to the nursing home asking for more information, but they had not replied. She said now there was to be a Social Services strategy meeting the following month with the Associate Director of the nursing home's parent company (the same man I and my sister had met early on), herself and her manager. At this meeting the Associate Director would have to say what had happened.

I asked her for a copy of the report once the strategy meeting had taken place and she said she could see no reason why not as it related to my mother, but she would check and get back to me. She told me she was now going on holiday and would be back in 10 days' time. She also said that the Associate Director had admitted that 'they didn't respond as they should have done.'

Thirteen days later we spoke again. She told me that the strategy meeting was now scheduled for the following week but the Associate Director had not yet confirmed his attendance. I asked what would happen if he did not attend; would the meeting go ahead? She said it would not go ahead without him and if he was uncooperative she would expect the CQC Inspector to decide what to do next.

Two and a half months passed. When I finally rang the Team Leader again I was astounded to hear that the person I had been dealing with was no longer on the case. The receptionist said that a Michael Smith had taken over from her. I asked her to give him a message, which was to ring me. She pulled up Mum's name on the computer and said that Mum's information had been passed on to him.

Michael Smith rang me two days later. He was surprised that I wanted information as he said he had not had anything about Mum passed onto him. He said he would have to retrieve Mum's file as it had gone to another department.

Three days later he rang me again. He had retrieved Mum's file and told me that the strategy meeting had been called to discuss one fracture, but not the second. He read to me the chronological events over the phone. The planned strategy meeting had finally taken place in November. I asked what things had been put in place to prevent an accident like this happening again. He told me that the home had not been asked to do anything different as there had been no abuse or neglect. I told him what the Associate Director had told me and my sister about the staff member not crossing the straps at the back of the hoist. 'Isn't that neglect?' I asked. He did not answer.

My frustration was mounting by the minute. I asked to receive a copy of the minutes of the strategy meeting. I told him how saddened I was that the cause of injury had not been explored as, if the staff at the home had used the sling properly in the first place Mum would not have needed to go into hospital. She would in all likelihood still have been alive at this moment.

I sensed that he thought the case was done and dusted as he asked me if I wanted anything else. Anything else? I had received nothing I wanted after all this time. I told him that, yes, I did want a number of very important things. I wanted to know exactly what had happened, and I wanted the Care Quality Commission to know that the home had been at fault because of the hoist; I wanted to know why, given my mother had had the accident in March and passed away in June, the strategy meeting had not happened until November. Michael agreed this was unusual. I told him that I was aware that the previous Safeguarding Team Leader had had difficulty getting the Associate Director of the nursing home company to attend any meeting as she had told me this herself. Silently, I had been surprised that the CQC did not have powers to insist that he attended.

I told Michael I was disappointed that the Safeguarding Team Leader had not kept the communication going between herself and me and I asked him to send me a copy of their complaints procedure, which he agreed to do.

Then I tried another approach and asked if he had seen the accident report and whether the home had made a formal report under the Reporting of Injuries, Diseases and Dangerous Occurrences Regulations (RIDDOR, 1995). He did not give a response to either question. (This was before we got the documentation that I described in the previous chapter. We only received that after two years.)

The strategy meeting minutes told us that a staff member employed by the home and a member of staff from an outside agency had been present when Mum sustained her injuries. The minutes seemed to contradict what we had been told by the Associate Director and I sent a letter to Michael explaining this.

Michael prevaricated. In response to my letter I got a holding letter that told me: 'As I am sure you will appreciate, the issues raised are complex and detailed. I will need to consult with those involved at the time of the incident in order to answer your points.'

A follow-up letter, three-and-a-half weeks later, gave better news. It told us the Social Services Strategy meeting was to be reconvened, with representatives of the nursing home company and Care Quality Commission to be in attendance. It was to be in seven weeks' time and we were invited to attend, either in person or by speaker-phone. That set us thinking about which option to choose. We needed to discuss what would serve us best and what we could cope with. The meeting at the hospital to discuss neglectful care there had been exceedingly stressful, and unsatisfactory, which suggested speaker-phone might be best, but discussing this when Keith, Ann and I lived so far apart was far from easy.

By the time we had made our decision I had heard again. In a letter dated 12 July I was told that the meeting had been cancelled and that this was partly our fault for not responding to the invitation sooner. An additional factor was that the Associate Director of the nursing home company was leaving his job. I was furious – though I could see we should have got back to Michael sooner – and wrote back, explaining our situation. I finished:

As a family we remain completely unsatisfied with the explanation we have received as to our late mother's injuries and are confused about the conflicting information we have been given on how these injuries happened. It is unfortunate that the Director of the Nursing Home Company is leaving/has left. However, we feel this should not mean that the cause of the accident cannot be looked into again. This should also not prevent the home and/or the staff member from the nursing agency from being reprimanded for what happened. We remain dissatisfied and would like clarification on how the injuries were sustained. I look forward to hearing from you.

Michael's letter in response gave us no satisfaction. He told us that the meeting had been cancelled partly because of our delay in replying, but also because the other parties were not in the end available. The CQC had declined to attend because they did not think the home had breached any regulations, while the Associate Director of the home was about to leave the company. Furthermore: 'The home is now in the hands of the administrator and the matron, manager and staff members present at the time of the accident are no longer in the employ of the nursing home. It is beyond my power to ensure any disciplinary action is taken against ex-employees of the nursing home. It is furthermore beyond my power to contact these individuals to further question them about the incident.'

So as far as Michael was concerned, that was that.

I rang to speak to the Care Quality Commission Inspector, Sarah, and left a message as she was not there. In response, I received a call from Jeff Jacobs (another CQC Inspector), who told me Sarah was no longer the Inspector for the area. He apologised for not being familiar with Mum's case and as the CQC's IT system was down he couldn't access any files. He said he would ring me on the following Wednesday, which he did. He had not been able to get Mum's file and would ring me the following week. After that, Jeff and I kept missing each other for a bit but finally we managed a telephone conversation. Jeff had now got a copy of the report from the strategy meeting and he went through it. I pointed out that the meeting had been in November and there was no evidence that the action points had been completed. I also pointed out a few inaccuracies in the report.

I asked Jeff if he had a copy of the home's original accident report and he said he had. He read it to me over the phone: it sounded very similar, if not identical, to that included in the strategy meeting minutes. (I thought to myself that it must have been re-written since originally being produced, as I recalled one of the managers/directors saying it was hard to read at our meeting in March the previous year). Jeff said that he could not understand why there had been a delay in the Care Quality Commission getting the accident report and then informing Social Services via confidential fax of the accident.

I felt as though I was going round in circles. With the constant changes in personnel and the inexplicable divisions in responsibilities it was becoming quite clear that I would never get to the bottom of the situation. Jeff suggested that I write to Michael and copy him in. I said I would and we ended the call.

With the nursing home in administration I had hit a brick wall in calling the former Associate Director, the Manager and the staff involved to account. The thought they were still 'out there' managing and providing the care of older people made me very angry. I corresponded with the administrators of the home for some time by letter, email and telephone, but achieved nothing.

It was two years after Mum had sustained the injuries in the nursing home that I learned the former Associate Director was now Director of a new company – a care agency. Armed with this information I tried to find it on the internet. Each time I typed in the new name the search engine referred to the website of the business that had owned and run my mother's nursing home before it went into administration. Finally, I typed in 'care agencies' for that area and there it was: the new business. Excited,

I texted my sister to say I would ring the agency the next day in the hope they were still at the address given.

I rang the care agency as planned and my suspicions were confirmed. It was essentially the same organisation that was still operating and the former Associate Director was still connected with it. I asked to speak to him and was told he would be back shortly. I told them why I was ringing and was promised he would ring me on returning to the office at 4 pm. I asked the woman I was speaking to to ring me to let me know even if he refused to speak to me. She said she would.

Having heard nothing, I rang again at 4.35 pm and was told that the Director had been 'taken home'. The receptionist did not say why and I did not ask. She added that anything to do with the nursing home needed to go through the administrators. She said that the Director would be off for the next two weeks.

This looked like definite avoidance to me, but I was determined to call those responsible for my mother's injuries to account. I discussed this in a detailed letter to the Care Quality Commission, including names and associated addresses where I could.

They wrote back promptly. It was a long letter and it told me one of the two pieces of information that I had been needing to hear. The new care agency was also no longer operating. I was not given a reason. I was not surprised, but I was angry. Now I had no way of contacting the nursing home Associate Director to find out what had really happened to Mum. He had slipped through the net again!

The Care Quality Commission also said, 'Information about those involved has been passed on to the CQC Inspectors and they may take the information into account when auditing those services'. Fair enough, but it seemed to me the individuals concerned were free to carry on as before.

Chapter 22

Preparing to make a claim

I awoke after a few hours' sleep looking back on what had happened to Mum. I thought about what was happening to vulnerable individuals in older people's services now, and worried about what I had seen on the news. I dragged myself out of bed and into the shower. I didn't want to, but I needed to focus on getting my NVQ candidates through their qualification. I tried to ignore feeling physically sick, not sure if it was because of the ongoing effects of my bereavements or just my concern about what I might find when I went to assess my NVQ candidates in their places of work.

I had not realised how hard it would be to drop the case, to no longer have the hope of finding out what exactly had happened to Mum and which agencies had let her down. The anger kept hitting me and I realised I couldn't let it drop after all. As a family, we decided that I should try again, this time asking for compensation to see if that would get a more satisfactory response. I got out my overflowing folder of documentation and started to put a letter together to the hospital.

The solicitor I had consulted had advised that a case could be brought against the nursing home for the fractures and the grade 2 pressure sore and the hospital for letting this develop into a grade 4 pressure sore, but all the other issues would have to be put on one side; there could be no redress. I hoped that if I made a claim as a lay person I could also include the poor practices and neglect by the staff, and the poor management. I hoped that we would go to court and I could face the people who had hurt my mother, and ask them why they had done it. It was not about money, it was about getting the story out there. (You may be wondering why I did not go to the media, but this is a difficult thing for people in the care sector to do. Throughout my career I had always been told that if anything happened at work we must not talk to the press. It is hard to go against something that has been drummed into you for many years.)

The letter to the hospital would be a difficult one to compose; it would be very complicated as so many people had contributed to my mother's terrible experience. It would also involve my reliving the nightmare we had been through. But I knew it had to be done.

Chapter 23

The good and the bad

I awoke the next morning. It had been a dream but it felt so real; I had been talking with Aunty Ann, and I had been able to ask her important questions and tell her how much I loved and missed her. She asked me how could someone with failing powers communicate what they wanted when they could no longer speak for themselves. 'Power of attorney,' I told her and as I played back the dream during the day I could not work out why Aunty Ann would have asked me this. She had been able to say what she wanted.

After my dream, I felt warm and comforted throughout the day – a lovely feeling. Love you Aunty Ann xx.

I signed in in the visitors' book and I went into the dining room with my NVQ candidate, Terry. Terry was asked to translate what an individual was saying as another staff member could not understand her. Terry and I turned around and as I looked at the individual a sudden rush of emotion filled me and jumped from the pit of my stomach to my throat. The lady was almost my late mother's double. I looked away and back again, away and back again. Yes, it was someone who could have been my mother's twin. My eyes welled up, I swallowed hard, again and again until I had regained my composure.

Terry crouched down so he was at the same level as the lady

and looked at her and asked what he could do for her. The lady responded in a mumble and Terry was able to translate and tell his colleagues what she wanted. Terry asked the lady if there was anything else he could do for her; she shook her head from side to side indicating that there wasn't. Terry said to her, 'I'm going into the quiet room now with my NVQ Assessor, Suzan, but if you want anything, come and get me, Okay?' and the lady nodded. I smiled at her as she looked up at me and inside I said, 'It's you, isn't it, Mum? No it can't be, but it is…'

In the quiet room, I gave positive feedback to Terry on how he had crouched down to be at eye level with her and then interpreted for her, checking back with her that that was what she had meant.

'What can be put in place for the lady to communicate more independently and for people to understand her?' I asked him.

'It's Okay. I can understand her and, like you saw, if there is a problem the staff call for me,' he told me.

'Yes, but you can't always be around, Terry, and I'm sure the lady would like to communicate without waiting for someone to interpret for her.'

'Do you mean something like a "talk board"?' he asked.

'Perhaps the speech therapist could work with the lady and they could both decide what's best for her.'

'I see what you mean. How do we get hold of the speech therapist?'

'The GP will need to make a referral. Why not go and mention it to your manager?' I prompted. And I followed him to the manager's office. The manager agreed the lady could do with speech therapy and suggested that Terry contact the GP for the referral.

'Brilliant. This will also be good NVQ evidence, Terry,' I told him and he looked really pleased.

'I'll go and tell her,' he said.

'Tell her – or ask her – if she wants you to contact her GP,' I added.

'Ask her of course, Suzan,' and we smiled, and Terry went to talk to the lady.

At the end of the session, I signed out in the visitors' book and tried not to look to my left as that was where my mother's 'twin' was. I felt spooked and wanted to ring family and tell them, but tell them what? Without seeing the lady for themselves they would not experience the impact of her being so much like Mum.

I went to see Simon, my other candidate. He had his NVQ folder out along with crisps and a drink.

'Hi Simon, how's you?' I asked as I put my bag on the table.

'Yeah, good thanks, Suzan, although I had trouble completing the assignment. I have to be honest and say I'm sorry, but there's some of it I couldn't do.'

'That's okay. We'll have a look at it together,' I said reassuringly, as it was not his fault that he hadn't received adequate training on the subject of the assignment. This was to understand what is abuse, how to prevent it and how to report any concerns he might have. He should have received this training, from his employer, within three months of being in post; as it was, he had been in post nearly a year when we were doing this.

Simon was a kind, caring and supportive man. I liked observing him for this NVQ. The way the individuals were drawn to him was brilliant. He afforded dignity and respect and saw the best in everyone. This last assignment did present him with a problem. I realised in our meeting that Simon was finding it difficult to hear that some people, whether it be the public, family, staff, clergymen, police officers, doctors or nurses, could abuse people, either intentionally or unintentionally. He could not believe that people could do bad things to other people. I knew I had tarnished his vision of the care sector and I apologised, but he needed to know that this negative side existed. For the NVQ unit on Protection he needed to research lessons learnt from past mistakes and he was shocked when he read about what Dr Shipman had done to older people, and the abuse that Victoria Climbier and Baby P had suffered.

Walking out of the door, I saw the 'rag n bone' man on his cart that was being pulled by a horse. It brought back memories of my childhood. I took some photos and gave the memory card to the manager of the next 'service' I was at; she printed them off. The photos would be used for discussion with the older individuals using the service.

I then went to another service to do some NVQ assessing. It was a lovely ride in the country and the sun was shining. I glanced across to the other side of the road and there were two hearses and a few cars following. I felt for them on their lonely way along the dual carriageway. We had done that for my aunt's funeral: funeral service in one area and the cremation in another about 10 miles away. It had felt like a lonely drive, but we were with my aunt all the way. We had gone all the way with Mum as well. The flood gates opened, but I told myself that I needed to be able to see to drive. Somehow I managed to get things under control. Through my tears I was cussing my Aunty Ann: 'Why didn't you tell us you were poorly if you knew?' (We had learned she had had cancer only after she had died.) And then in my head I talked to her to tell her how much I missed her, and I told myself that she was no longer in pain.

I delivered some completed NVQ portfolios and congratulation cards for those who had successfully completed their qualification. The manager asked how the others were progressing and I said the majority were doing well, but one of the staff who was doing an NVQ was not working to the standard required for a senior care worker.

Some managers try to insist you get their staff through, but this was a positive manager who said she would discuss the issue with the candidate. She did just that and found the candidate was unable to take on any responsibility for what he did or mistakes that he made. For example, he was asked to read and complete a piece of work but because the side of the paper he was looking at was not the side he needed he would blame someone else for the information not being available rather than thinking to turn over the paper and see the other side. After an action plan had been put in place and then not completed, the manager took that candidate off the NVQ programme. I had great respect for her.

At a different service I walked up to my NVQ candidate who was staring out of the window. My eyes followed hers and I didn't like what I saw. An older, frail individual was walking in the garden, on a bumpy surface with stones and gravel stopping her walking frame from moving forward. She was clearly in trouble as she tried to move it. Any minute she would fall over. I was really shocked when one of my NVQ candidates turned around and said, 'I'm not going to report it. You can report it if you want to, but I'm not. They don't listen anyway.'

'But you have a duty of care, which means you must report any concerns you have,' I said. 'And not only is it your duty, but it is also part of the NVQ unit on Health, Well-being and Protection. You have to demonstrate that you will report concerns.'

'I'm not going to,' she replied adamantly.

I could have stayed and tried to persuade her, but the safety of the older person was more important. I went outside to help her back into the building. Later I reported my concerns to the manager, and also the troubling fact that the NVQ candidate would not report it.

I went back to that candidate. 'We need to discuss this with your manager as just now you demonstrated that you won't report things that concern you.'

'I just do my job and go home afterwards,' was all she said as she leant against the wall.

'I'll leave it to the manager to tell us what she wants to happen,'

I told her as I walked away. That staff member never completed her NVQ.

Later I sat in with a staff member and another of my NVQ candidates and watched a training DVD on abuse. The DVD taught us what abuse was and how to report it. There was nothing to complete at the end of watching it to find out what we had learnt. Just because someone has watched a DVD, or has sat in on a trainer-led training course, you cannot assume that person has taken in what has been said.

I asked both the candidate and the other staff member what they would do if their manager abused or neglected an individual. The staff member answered before my NVQ candidate, 'I don't know.' My NVQ candidate then told her what to do. 'You should inform the manager above her or contact the Care Quality Commission, or AGE UK, or The Link,' she said. ('The Link' is now called 'Healthwatch'.)

Although I found the DVD useful, I am a trainer in Protection from Abuse and know quite a bit about it so most of it was repetition for me. At the same time, it had seemed to me that, had I been new to the care profession, the DVD would have left me with some unanswered questions. And it certainly would have been better if a senior member of staff could have been in the room to answer any questions new staff might have. Even better would have been to watch it in a classroom setting with other people, to discuss and share thoughts.

This service had a coded fastening for the front door. The entry code to get in was given to staff, relatives, district nurses, doctors and so on. I asked how often the codes were changed and the staff did not know. One member of staff said that the code had not been changed for at least six months.

A few weeks before I had been waiting near the lounge for an NVQ candidate when the front door had opened and a nurse had run through the hall and up the stairs. Running was dangerous and expressly forbidden so I was not impressed about that, but I was also shocked that she had not signed in in any way. When I brought what I had seen to the attention of a senior member of staff, she said it was okay as the nurses were always in a rush and that's why they had to have the code to the front door. I did not like the fact that someone was in the building who had not signed in in the visitor's book or told anyone she was there.

My brother-in-law's mother had a key code on her front door and on one occasion when I called in to see her I found a brightly coloured piece of paper on her door step. I took it in and gave it to her and we found that it was a professional carer's list of key codes to get into all her clients' houses. We were both appalled. The carer had not tried to retrace her steps to find it. My sister took it into the office of the agency that organised this service.

Chapter 24

Preparing to go to court

I wanted our case against the hospital to go to court. I needed what had happened to be discussed in a courtroom so everyone could hear about the shocking things that had happened to my mother, and how she had been let down by those who had had a professional duty to protect her. I wanted the opportunity to ask questions. I also wanted a public apology, not a private 'sorry' in a confidential letter to me.

In preparation, I visited a court and sat in the public gallery for several cases. There were cases of murder, shootings, and rape; one case related to sexual abuse of older women in a care home. I wanted to sit in on this to find out why someone might sexually abuse (or abuse in any way) older, vulnerable people.

This particular case was of a male care worker who was accused of sexually abusing older women who lived in the care home where he worked. As I listened, I gasped aloud when the judge did the summing up and said things like: 'He put his hand up Mrs A's dress and tugged down her knickers. He told her to go to the toilet and check her pad. Before she was in the toilet he felt her backside. He claims he was trying to feel if she was wet.

'He put his hand down the front of Mrs B's skirt and into her underwear. On another occasion, after he had given Mrs B a bath and was drying her, Mrs B said that he tickled her where he shouldn't have. In between her legs, she added.'

The judge told the jury that he was going to adjourn the case whilst they considered if the care worker was guilty of those offences.

Spending time in court gave me some idea of the layout and what the procedure was and how I and my family would be cross-examined. As we had decided not to work with the solicitor, I would be representing myself. I informed the family that they would be called as witnesses. I had read somewhere that you should never give too much away in court but instead should listen carefully to what is being said and only answer what you are being asked. A very simple example would be, if you are asked the question 'Are you wearing a watch?' you might infer that you were being asked for the time, but the question is not asking for the time, it is asking only if you are wearing a watch. Now I needed to follow this preparation through.

Chapter 25

My letter of claim

In response to my claim and accompanying letter to the hospital I received a holding email telling me the claim had been passed to the NHS Litigation Authority (NHSLA), who handle all claims for clinical negligence.

It was four months before I heard from the NHSLA. When a reply came it was disappointing. Analysing the wording I realised it dealt only with the pressure sore and on this point it said that the staff had followed the accepted standards, although not all the time.

I was forced to write again. Why, I asked, had there been no specific pressure ulcer prevention care plan in the nursing documentation? Why had Mum's ulcer not been formally assessed when she was admitted, given that this was a requirement within six hours of admission? And why, when Mum's ulcer was supposed to be formally assessed every three days had this not happened on 21 occasions? (The letter from the NHSLA did admit this was 'not acceptable practice', but they did not say why it had happened or what had been done to improve things since.)

Why, I asked, when good practice dictated that my mother should have been nursed on a pressure-relieving mattress from the day of her admission due to her pre-existing grade 2 pressure ulcer, had this not been done? (Sadly there was no documentary evidence available in my mother's notes to support this.) And finally (as far as the pressure sore was concerned), why had the 'turning programme' for preventing further sores not been followed? In my mother's notes, there was a 'turn-chart' (a record of when my mother was repositioned to vary areas of pressure) that was commenced on the day of admission, but the frequency of repositioning had varied unacceptably in practice: while the chart required she be turned every two hours, this had happened only on occasions; on one occasion she had been left for nine hours and on others it had varied between three and six hours.

And then there were all the issues the NHSLA had not addressed at all. In particular, I reminded them that the hospital had failed to follow the guidelines and standards set out in the Department of Health's End of Life Care Strategy document: *Promoting high quality care for all adults at the end of life* (Department of Health 2008, www.gov.uk/government/publications/end-of-life-care-strategy-promoting-high-quality-care-for-adults-at-the-end-of-their-life)

The NHSLA responded a second time by saying that they had carried out an in-depth investigation and were satisfied that the standards for pressure sore care had been met. Meanwhile, failure to follow the guidelines and standards of the End of Life Care Strategy and the other areas of poor practice should be dealt with via the complaints procedure. In other words, in the NHSLA's view (and, you will remember, the view of the solicitor whom I had consulted) only the pressure sore neglect amounted to medical negligence and could be the subject of a claim. All the other elements of poor practice had to follow a different procedure that was not designed for cases of medical negligence. I had of course already tried this route and met a brick wall.

I had clear evidence in my mother's notes that standards had not been followed. As a family we now had to decide whether to risk our homes, should our case fail, and take the NHS to court. To help make this difficult decision, I contacted another solicitor I knew on Facebook for her informal advice:

> *Hi Jane, I hope you don't mind me asking this question? I know*
> *negligence is not your area but I wonder if you can help. I sent*
> *a Letter of Claim to the NHS re negligence and got a letter back*
> *from the Litigation Team saying that there is no claim. I know*
> *there is and wish to progress it. I am a lay person and need to*
> *pursue this case personally, for my late Mum and my family. I*
> *have a care background and know the legislation that surrounds*
> *care, but don't know much on the process of making a claim. I*
> *would be very grateful if you could tell me what I need to do*
> *next – that is, should I write back to the Litigation Team or get in*
> *touch with the court and register my claim? Are there any case*
> *studies of a lay person suing the NHS? Many thanks in advance*
> *for your help, Suzan*

She replied immediately, asking for my phone number and telling me I could make use of the free consultation her firm offered with someone expert in the field, to give me pointers to pursue. I gave her my number and she put me in touch with a solicitor (John) who she thought could help me.

John rang me. I told him the full story of how the hospital had failed in its duty of care towards Mum. I explained how I had been brushed off with regard to my claim for medical negligence and how I now thought my best approach would be to make a claim under the Human Rights Act Articles 2 & 3. These are (Article 2) the right to life and (Article 3) the prohibition of torture and inhuman or degrading treatment or punishment.

I said that while I knew the hospital had not deliberately caused serious suffering, some of the treatment my mother had endured had been akin to torture, and had caused intense physical and mental suffering. (I knew that an individual's situation had to meet a minimum level of severity and I assumed putting my mother on her back with the catheter pipe pressing into the grade

4 pressure sore would meet that level. www.legislation.gov.uk/
ukpga/1998/42/schedule/1)

John listened to my account without rushing me. That felt
good. He said that a claim under the Human Rights Act would
need to be done in Strasbourg, but the horrid things Mum had
endured *would* come under medical negligence. As the NHSLA
team were refusing to admit anything had been done wrong,
legal action was my only option. However, he warned me, 'The
Litigation team may offer a Without Prejudice payment, but they
won't admit liability.'

I already knew what that meant: offering a sum of money
without admitting they had done anything wrong. It shocked me
that they would not formally admit to what had happened even
though I had written correspondence from the hospital apologis-
ing for a lot of problems.

He asked me what I wanted to achieve, which was a very
useful question after all this time. I told him it was not about
receiving money for the harm my mother had suffered; it was
about putting things right. So, did I want to go to court, he questioned? It was highly unlikely it would ever get far enough for
me to pose any of the questions I had been hoping to ask. That
put the situation in a very different light. Understanding this for
the first time, I no longer wanted it to go to court. He had made
me realise that I had done all that I could.

Not wanting to rush me, he gave me his telephone number
and said I could ring him if I thought of any more questions after
I had put the phone down. He would not charge for this – he just
wanted to help. I felt such relief.

I emailed Jane to thank her: 'It was just what I needed, a
solicitor that was happy to give advice and also to listen. I feel a
whole weight has been lifted and I am clear again on which route
I now want to go.'

Where I wanted to go now was to pursue a mission – my mission to raise standards and improve care for vulnerable people. This would need all my energy and spare time. It was time to make something positive out of the past.

. . . .

If you are facing a similar dilemma:

- Surf the internet and arrange a free half-hour consultation with a solicitor who deals with medical negligence. This can be face to face or on the telephone.
- Make notes before you attend the appointment.
- There is no rule to say that you cannot visit several solicitors for free consultations.
- Get support for yourself.
- Do not talk to colleagues, friends and acquaintances about what has happened as this could confuse things. You might say the wrong thing or you might accidentally include what these people have said in your statements.

Chapter 26

Loss

'You'll know, won't you, Suzan?' the Deputy Manager said as I arrived at the service.

'Know what?' I asked as I took off my coat and signed the visitors' book.

'If it's true that you can die from a broken heart?'

'I've read that the stress and shock of losing someone suddenly can cause heart failure. The risk of a cardiac arrest is many times higher the day after losing a spouse.'

'See, told you,' the Deputy Manager told the staff member who had wanted to know this.

'I knew a lady who said she never, ever wanted to go into a residential home,' I said. 'Unfortunately, whilst living in sheltered accommodation, it became clear she needed more support. The day she moved into a care service, she died. "Natural causes," the doctor said.'

'That's awful,' remarked the staff member.

'A person moving into a care or nursing home loses a lot of things – their home, most of their furnishings, things that are familiar to them, neighbours popping in; having their own front door, their own garden, their own privacy, their own animals, a reasonable amount of space. And their double bed becomes more often than not a single bed in a care or nursing home,' I said.

'Yeah, why is that?' the staff member asked.

'To help with hoisting,' I told her.

'What about those who don't need hoisting? Could they have a double bed?' The staff member looked at me and I looked at the Deputy Manager.

'They can if they ask for one,' she replied.

'Do you tell people, either on admission or when they're looking around, that they can have a double bed if they want one?' I asked.

'No. Many of the rooms aren't big enough,' the Deputy Manager admitted.

'Another loss is when staff leave the home to work elsewhere or do other things, or when another individual in the service passes away. All this is loss. It is a major change and can affect the person the same way as a bereavement does; staff and family need to be aware of this,' I told them.

The Deputy Manager added, 'We need to support individuals with loss. For example, once staff have decided to leave, we need to tell the individuals in the home so they have time to come to terms with it. If an individual is dying, whilst giving dignity and respect to the dying, we need to inform the other individuals and ask if they want to talk about it, and/or say their "goodbyes".'

A staff member asked if I had five minutes, and could we have a chat. Of course I said we could, after the NVQ assessment I had come for. During the assessment, I could hear an older lady asking a staff member nervously, 'What do you want me to do next? I'm new here. I only moved in today. I don't know what to do...' A staff member quietly reassured her as they walked out into the garden.

After the NVQ assessment I found the staff member who wanted to talk and we went to a quiet area of the service. The staff member was quite reserved, which was unusual for her, so I knew something was wrong. She asked me if she could tell me something and asked me not to tell anybody else. I said I could not decide this until she had told me what it was and if it was anything about harm to an individual using the service, then I would need to report it.

She said that a resident had passed away whilst she was delivering personal care. He was very poorly and his passing was expected. She went on to say that she knew she had no right to be upset because she had only known him for a year and other staff had known him for a lot longer. I was shocked to hear her say she 'had no right to be upset' and discussed this with her, saying that although she had only known him for a year, I was sure that the way she had provided care with dignity and respect was to a high standard and that this man would have felt valued and respected.

As we talked some more, it became apparent that the Manager had asked the majority of staff how they were feeling after the death, but had not asked her. She again said, 'I know I have no right, but it was my first death...' I advised her to ask the Manager or Deputy for some time to talk it through and she laughed, but not in a happy way. I said perhaps she could ask for a supervision session with her manager. In response to that she asked me if I knew what her supervisions were like and I replied that I did not. She said that she received a form sent in the post to her home address asking if she had any problems and to sign the form and put it back in the post; that is all her supervision consisted of.

I told her that she should have regular, planned one-to-one private supervision sessions with her manager and that these should do a number of very important things. They should identify her strengths and weaknesses and any training needs, and thereby support her development. Without this, how was she to learn and improve? They should ensure she carried out her duties effectively and in line with the General Social Care Codes of Practice, and review her workload and the variety of tasks given to her so that she had the right tools and competencies to do her job. Very importantly, she needed the opportunity to reflect on her practice so she could maintain good practice and improve. Unfortunately, ensuring this happened was outside my remit. I could only tell her what should be in place. It would be up to her to discuss it with her manager or follow the complaints procedure.

This member of staff had experienced her first death as a care worker and it had hit her hard. 'I cried,' she told me. She had had a good relationship with the individual and had really cared about him.

'You were with him when it mattered most to him,' I told her. 'You're a good care worker with good skills, knowledge and compassion. Just by being with him and letting him know you cared about him was the most important thing.'

I had been fortunate. Few people close to me, or who I worked with or supported, had passed away. In my 20-plus years of supporting people with learning disabilities, I had experienced three deaths. I was shocked to realise how many older people had died in the older people's services that I was visiting to assess staff. I took my hat off to the staff who coped with this on the outside very well, aware that perhaps inside they were an emotional mess, as I would have been. Outwardly they maintained a professional stance.

Being an NVQ Assessor, I was there for my NVQ candidates, but as other staff and individuals got to know me I found they too shared their feelings with me. I noticed some individuals would say to each other, 'Oh, here she is. Go and tell her,' and they would come and tell me things that were on their minds when other staff were not around. If they didn't come back to me, I discreetly went to them before I left the service again.

I was told of many problems, and these made me think of my

mother and the care I had wanted and expected for her:

'Staff come into my bedroom during the night, checking on me.'

'I don't like how staff talk loudly to me. I am not deaf.'

'The food is lovely, but they give me too much.'

'I moved in 16 days ago and I haven't been taken out yet.'

I had to advise them to tell a member of staff or the Manager and I would go with them if they wanted me to. Being an observer on the outside can be a difficult thing.

Chapter 27

If I could only bottle these visits...

I was sitting in the dining room waiting for my NVQ candidate to finish what she was doing. Whilst waiting, I took in what was happening in this room. There was quiet talk between various people at different tables. It was happy talk. One mother was telling her daughter how happy she was living there. Another lady, with dementia, was being supported by a staff member. Another was being quietly helped into her wheelchair and leaving the room. Staff spoke at a level that the individual could hear. I was good at picking up on body language and at that moment I could say that the individuals using the service, staff and the relatives – everyone in that room at that particular time – were happy to be at the home and happy with the service.

Fortunately my NVQ candidate came along and distracted me from other memories.

Three days later I was back at this service to see a different candidate. He told me how he had supported a lady that morning with end-of-life care. Those words hit me hard and it took me back to the poor end-of-life care my mother had received when she was dying.

The candidate told me he 'felt privileged' to give personal care to a lady who was confined to bed and leaving this world. Why, oh why, could Mum not have had someone like him to help her when she was dying in hospital? I swallowed hard and told him how lovely that was. He took it in his stride; he didn't realise how good he was at his job and how much the people he supported valued him.

A week or so later I was assessing how a candidate administered medication. Previously we had planned which individual I hoped to observe her.

'We're short staffed today,' the NVQ candidate told me. 'Well, no, that's not true. We have our usual quota, which is never enough, but we have a resident who's dying. We don't have extra staff to sit with people when they're dying, but I have pulled one of the staff off the floor and asked her to sit with the lady concerned. I will not have anyone dying alone.'

I observed my candidate follow the medication procedure; she knocked on the bedroom door of Beryl, asked if Beryl was happy for me to observe, and explained why. Beryl said I could and I was invited in. I walked quietly and slowly into the room. I felt I was intruding, but Beryl had understood what would be happening and had agreed to my being there. She was in bed and looked very frail. A lump jumped into my throat as I could see she was very ill and her life would end soon. Then tears welled up in my eyes as I observed my candidate administer the medication gently and caringly; she spoke to the lady in one of the most caring ways I had ever heard. Beryl looked straight into her eyes and they both smiled at each other. Beryl thanked my candidate and she stroked Beryl's arm.

I thanked Beryl, left the room and composed myself in the hall. I followed my candidate downstairs; she seemed on a mission as she was walking quite fast. Having said that, all staff tend to walk fast in the large services for older people; they have so much to do.

'There's a bird nesting in the drain pipe outside the window of Derek's room. He's one of the people who lives here. I've been taking photographs with my mobile phone. We shouldn't have our phones on but mine is always on silent,' she told me.

'What have you done with the photos?' I asked.

'I've been showing Derek. He's bedbound. He loves birds but can't turn his head to see the window and the bird.'

'Okay,' I replied, waiting for her to tell me more.

'But I've had an idea. I'm going to ask him if I can put a mirror on his chest of drawers and position it so he can see the reflection of the bird. Then he can see live what's happening.'

'Lovely idea,' I told her and wondered why all care staff could not be this thoughtful.

Chapter 28

Facing the future

'How people die remains in the memory of those who live on.'
Dame Cicely Saunders, Founder of the Modern Hospice
Movement

I had been really ill with the stress of trying to co-ordinate the follow-up with all the services that let Mum and the family down. At the same time, I was still going into older people's services, assessing and finding things wrong. I realised I could not cope any more.

I could not think ahead; I felt I had nothing to look forward to. I knew that grief affected the body in many ways and there were many factors involved. For example, when you lose someone, in addition to grief, you may feel anger and guilt. I knew that my anger with those who had hurt my mother, and my guilt because I had not been able to stop them, were together blocking the grieving process.

I was taking vitamin and mineral supplements as I knew that grief was a physical drain on my body; I hoped they would right the balance. At the same time, I was aware that I had started drinking a bit to dull the pain, to relax me and to get me to sleep. I needed a good night's sleep; two hours a night was not enough and did not let me function effectively the next day. I only had one or two glasses of wine (diluted heavily with lemonade) with dinner, but in the past I had usually had a drink only on special occasions as I did not really like it. I wished I did and then I could drink myself into oblivion.

All I could think about was what had happened to my mother. I had nothing left to offer friends or potential partners. I felt them drifting away from me. It was not intentional, but I was aware it was happening and could do nothing to stop it. I needed people who were kind, caring and understanding, not people telling me to stop this crusade and get on with my life. Why did they want to brush under the carpet all the bad things that were happening to older people? I felt isolated and that nobody understood my fight to get these things sorted. People, including friends who were also professionals, told me to leave it alone and move on; I had told them what had happened but they said things like, 'The staff were very busy; they work long hours.' I knew this, but I couldn't understand why they didn't think it was important to try to put things right. How I coped with all this did not always make me popular.

My short-term memory went. My eating pattern changed and I knew that I was over-eating – comfort eating. I cancelled quite a bit of work, explaining about the ongoing effects of my double bereavement (my aunt and my mother); I felt that people thought I was making it up. I had also verbally agreed a contract to write some books; fortunately I had not got around to signing it. I realised that I could not think about anything apart from losing Mum and Aunty Ann. Everything else was insignificant.

Mornings were the worst; there were many when I did not want to get up and I dreaded the day ahead. I cried. Generally, as the day went on I would begin to feel better and by the evening I would feel not 100 per cent but 'okay'. Sometimes, because I was feeling well in the evening, I would make plans to meet up with friends the following day. I did not do this too often as I soon learnt that I could not manage to follow it through. Some understood; some did not.

'You should be over it by now,' some said. I had lost many friends, but perhaps they were never real friends in the first place.

I had paid privately to see a bereavement counsellor. I saw her twice and did not go again. I did not feel we were suited and at the time I was still fighting the case, and was not ready for counselling.

My nerves were affected; I felt 'jumpy'. Sometimes it felt as though someone was right behind me when I was standing still, such as when I was at the sink washing up. Or when I was alone in bed there were some nights when I thought someone was on the other side of the door. Of course, I knew there was no one there; it was the anxiety making me think it in the first place. I was also unable to stop and work out the risks and consequences of doing something before I did it. This was very surprising as I have always had to assess risk as part of my job. It was just a little thing, but I noticed I would boil the kettle and not wait for it to switch itself off before I poured the hot water. I had never done that before.

On my birthday, one of my best friends passed away. She had been very tired during the day and had gone to bed for a few hours sleep but never woke up. I tried to cope with this shock, but the loss affected me deeply. My nerves were shattered and my anxieties came back in force.

I visited my GP, who was very understanding and knew about what I had been through. He did not judge; he listened. I told him I had had a complete meltdown where I had clenched my fists and fallen to the floor screaming. I said I needed something that would help me and he prescribed anti-depressants. He said that they would take a few weeks to work but they should help. It was true they took time to work, but when they did I felt great. I wasn't hyper or anything like that, but I no longer felt the pain, the sadness, the hurt and the tears.

At last I was able to look back on what had happened to my mother more objectively and no longer blame myself for not having been able to help her. I could now see that I had done all I could to raise my concerns with the nursing home management, the Safeguarding Team at Social Services, the hospital's Director of Nursing and the Care Quality Commission. I had also put my business at risk by taking so much time off work to be with Mum. What more could I have done? Thankfully, I was at last able to stop myself taking on the guilt.

I was really surprised by people's reactions when I told them I was on anti-depressants. I didn't tell many people, but of those I did, one health professional looked shocked and wrinkled her nose; another friend said sharply, 'You've got to cut them down!' I was only on one tablet a day, and I felt better than I had done for a long time now.

Over the years some Christmases had been family ones and some I had spent holidaying somewhere hot. Now it felt essential to have a family Christmas. My anxieties were such that I was convinced one of us was going to die and it would be our last Christmas all together.

Part of me understood I was experiencing a major depressive episode. Fortunately, the medication helped me to remain calm and enjoy a family Christmas day. I was there, but sometimes on the outside, looking in, analysing what people were doing, how they were laughing and how happy they looked. I wanted to get my camera out and take some photos, perhaps the last family photos I would take I thought morbidly, but I didn't.

Knowing that exercise released endorphins into the body which alleviated anxiety, I started yoga and Pilates. I also did a lot of walking. Once I had truly decided to give up on my claims, feeling I had achieved all I could, I began to feel relief. At last I felt able to start concentrating on what I could do to help people in a similar situation, and to prevent it happening to others.

If you find yourself in my place:

- Grief is very painful and is a normal part of being a human being.
- Give yourself time to grieve. Your workplace may give you some time off but it can take up to five years to go through the grieving process.
- Be aware that there may be things that will hinder or help your progress.
- Exercise and eat healthily.
- Consider taking vitamin and mineral supplements to help the body during this time (but if you are on prescribed medication, ensure you discuss this with your GP or the pharmacist as the supplements could interact with your prescribed medication).
- While it is important not to become dependent on them in the long term, anti-depressants really are worth considering to get you through a crisis.

Chapter 29

A care worker's concerns

Georgia, a care worker, contacted me to ask for my help. She said she had reported some concerns to the Care Quality Commission. In particular, she had reported a male staff member for leaving individuals in his care sitting in saturated pads. The CQC had visited the service for older people where she worked, as a result of her report, and had found that it was not achieving many of the essential standards for quality and safety.

Georgia told me that her manager was now picking on her work and had written to her, inviting her to a meeting and advising her to bring someone along for support. She asked me to go to this meeting and I agreed I would, even before she had explained why the meeting was happening. Having been a manager, I had held meetings like this to discuss why a staff member, despite receiving lots of support, was not performing or improving. The role of the 'support person' is to be present, but not to participate in the meeting.

We entered the office and I shook hands with the Manager and two other senior staff. The Manager explained that she would be writing notes and that everyone would receive a copy of what was said in the meeting. She said that she would write me down as a 'friend to the staff member'.

The Manager started talking about her concerns about some of the things that Georgia had done and should not have. These were trivial things, which in my opinion did not require such a meeting, and the Manager did not give Georgia time to speak. Georgia asked for clarification of what she had allegedly done or not done and the Manager ignored her.

I knew that my role as a 'support person' was to sit there quietly, but I felt it was only right that I spoke out. I told the Manager that she should listen to Georgia. The Manager waited whilst Georgia spoke, then quickly carried on with her agenda and did not reply to Georgia. I asked that evidence be provided to show that Georgia had done what the senior staff were accusing her of. The Manager asked the senior staff to produce the evidence; they said they did not have it with them as they had not known they would need it.

I asked for the meeting to be adjourned and reconvened if and when there was evidence to substantiate what was being claimed against Georgia. The Manager needed some convincing, but eventually agreed. It was obvious to me that she was not experienced in this area and I gave her my business card and left the office. Before leaving the home, I told Georgia how well she had done. She had been confident, polite and assertive throughout.

I asked her why she had not got in touch with the whistle-blowing charity 'Public Concern at Work' (website http://www.pcaw.org.uk/). It turned out she had not heard of it. I told her that when she received training on Safeguarding and Protecting people she should have been told that if she suffered harassment after raising a concern, then she should either contact her union, if she was in one, or contact the charity. I gave her the telephone number and asked her to put it in her phone, which she did.

The meeting was never reconvened.

Two days later I delivered a training workshop for the public on how to protect yourself or another older person when in care or in hospital, or living at home. I advised participants to make sure to keep in touch with family and friends, to avoid becoming isolated, as this could increase their vulnerability, and to tell someone, say the GP or a nurse, if they were worried.

I gave them this example: Every time you visit your friend in her nursing home, Dorothy (another individual there, aged 82), rushes up to you for a chat. Today, though, she walks slowly towards you. She has bruises on her forearms. Do you dismiss the bruises? And the unusual slow walking towards you? Do you put these things down to her getting old? Or do you do something different?

When the participants had discussed the options, we agreed on this response: she might have had a fall; she might have a pain in her back which is causing her to walk slowly. But you *do not know* and *you must not assume* that it is because she is old.

You can:

- Listen to the person concerned;
- Watch that person's body language;
- Watch what is going on around him/her;
- Visit frequently and vary the time you visit.

Most members of staff are not abusers and neglect and/or abuse is unintentional in most cases. Neglect and/or abuse happens for many reasons. Whatever these might be, you need to intervene and you need to complain.

Chapter 30

Turning guilt into positive action

Elisabeth Kubler-Ross, in her famous book on death and dying, has said that guilt may be the most painful companion of death. It took quite a while for me to realise that I had been blaming myself for not being able to do more for my mother. I should have visited more often, I told myself, forgetting how difficult that was; I should have spoken out more, forgetting how much I had tried to do but how little I had been listened to. Only with time to reflect could I begin to see that my mother's death had not been my fault. Mum had been in a nursing home and then a hospital, both of which had had a duty of care – a duty to protect her, a vulnerable person. The Social Services Safeguarding Team had also had a duty of care, and the Care Quality Commission.

I thought back to the nursing home, the meeting I had had with its management team, and the written information I had given to the Safeguarding Team leaders at Social Services. I thought too of the hospital, of the first meeting where my sister and I had told the Director of Nursing and the Ward Sister of our concerns; of the second meeting after Mum had passed away with the same Director of Nursing but a different Ward Sister who had kept saying 'sorry' but refused to write anything on the staff personnel records; she had at least had enough guts to sit in a room with us and hear how her staff had treated my mother.

In particular, I thought about the individuals – the nursing staff who had treated Mum well and those who had chosen not to listen to her or to me and who had, for whatever reason, caused Mum pain and harm. Why, I asked myself do people who have a duty of care give poor care, or neglect or even abuse a vulnerable older person? Is it a lack of training, or of supervision and support? Is it low pay and long hours owing to staff shortages and reduced budgets? Is it as simple as a lack of compassion and a person being in the wrong profession?

Older people can be vulnerable to poor treatment because their hearing or ability to think is impaired. A stroke or dementia may have made speech difficult. If they are in a situation where an abusive staff member is in a position of power – especially if, like my mother, they cannot walk – they may be too scared to speak out and their relatives and friends may believe healthcare professionals know the right way to do things and will not question their authority.

It is probably all of these, but what I am sure is that it is not a whole hospital or care home that gives poor care, it is the individual. And if that individual has not been trained, or properly supported, then the individuals who manage them are also responsible. Right the way up the chain of command, it is individuals that make a difference and if a manager does not keep an eye on what staff are doing, then the manager is at fault.

Individuals who see abuse and turn a blind eye must also bear responsibility. The GP or nurse who visits a service (or sees the older person at their surgery) and can tell things are not right but does not report it, must share the blame, as must volunteers, family or friends who know something is wrong but do nothing about it.

Whenever another case of abuse of older people in hospitals or care services is publicised in the media (and this is becoming increasingly frequent), those in charge say that 'lessons have been learned'. Do I believe that lessons have been learned? No, or at least not enough lessons and not sufficient learning. Abuse will continue and perhaps increase unless we, the public, make it sufficiently clear to national and local government, the institutions where older people are being cared for, and the individuals who care for them, that we will not accept poor current practices.

We hear about further cases of elder abuse in the news, but once the news has been aired that seems to be the end of it – until the next time. And then the same thing happens again. Why is more not being done to make people aware of the abuse taking place in hospitals, care services and people's own homes all the time?

I wrote to the Care Quality Commission asking for data on the number of Safeguarding alerts (reporting concerns) on people over the age of 65 for the period January to June 2012. They sent me detailed data, but the key fact was that in those six months alone there had been over 12,000 alerts. This is a shocking statistic in itself, but it includes only the reported cases. Many concerns go unreported because staff feel they might lose their job or be victimised or bullied if they speak up. Only recently I sat in as a 'support person' in a meeting where a staff member who was a whistle blower was victimised and accused of 'bringing shame onto the home'.

Unfortunately, it is quite common now to hear about health and care services not meeting the Essential Standards of Quality and Safety and also about homes closing owing to very poor standards. The reactive approach, where we wait for the Care Quality Commission to go in and audit the service and then act if needed, often leads to the older individuals affected enduring unacceptable standards and then suddenly having to move care/ nursing home at a time when change can be detrimental to them.

In summary, many older, vulnerable people are receiving poor levels of health and social care. They and/or their relatives and members of the public do not always know what is good or poor practice and what they can do about it, partly because they have never been told, and also because they have no point of comparison. Many councils provide training for their staff, but not for those receiving care or their relatives. People receiving services need to know what good and bad are. Knowledge is power. The staff have knowledge, therefore they have power. This power needs to be given to the older, vulnerable people receiving care. We need to change the reactive approach to a proactive one.

Talking about these issues will in itself make a difference. We need to talk about what is good practice and what is poor practice, and to acknowledge that neglect and abuse are possible anywhere, not just in the extreme cases reported in the media.

My mother's experience has left me with a mission. What I can do is to raise awareness and campaign for a raft of measures that I believe will promote good practice. What *you* can do is...

Chapter 31

What *you* can do

You may be a relative, a friend, the postman – you can become the advocate of an older, vulnerable person receiving care or in need of care. If you are concerned about them, or their care or treatment, please speak up. Even if everything turns out to be fine, at least you will have raised the issue and made it known that someone is watching out for that person. You may without knowing it have stopped something bad happening. Be observant and learn to recognise the warning signs of neglect and abuse and the risk factors (see www.spcconsultancy.com/abuse.html).

There are things you can do to prevent abuse. Build a network, so friends and family communicate with each other and can organise a visiting schedule. Staggered regular visits mean the person concerned will be seen regularly and will at the same time not be overwhelmed by everyone turning up altogether.

Many people who are not in the care profession have told me they have been unhappy with care or the standards of homes where a friend or relative lived, but have not known how to get things changed. In the Appendix I have included guidance on how to make an informal and a formal complaint about care. In doing this, remember the 'three Bs': be polite; be calm; be assertive but not aggressive. When someone receives a complaint, s/he should be thinking: 'How can I put this right?' Give her/him space to think this through. At the same time you must persist; do NOT assume that 'everything will be alright'.

Sometimes it can be harder if you are 'in the profession'. I received three telephone calls from different care workers in the same week asking me what they should do about concerns where they worked. I told them they had to start by following their company's complaints procedure or, if they felt unable to do that, report their concerns to the Care Quality Commission, (anonymously if they wished) and the CQC would follow it up. I was pleased subsequently to hear care workers in the homes concerned talking about getting a visit from the CQC Inspector.

> **Look around you**
> **Who is alone?**
> **Who is scared?**
> **THINK!**
> **What can I do about it?**

And remember, if you think an actual crime has been committed, you must contact the police.

Chapter 32

Why the health and social care system need not have failed my mother

My mother died as a result of a completely avoidable chain of events. Because a hoist was used incorrectly, she fell and broke both legs. Bad nursing both before and after she was admitted to hospital for the breaks meant she developed first a grade 2 and finally a grade 4 pressure sore that eventually caused blood poisoning. During her final days in hospital she was often needlessly in great pain, yet she, and we, her family, were shown little sympathy.

None of this need have happened. Yet while everything was unravelling, we, her family tried so hard to put things right. We had a meeting with the nursing home to try to find out how she had broken her legs. We met with the Director of Nursing at the hospital to try to get better care for her. My brother, sister, niece and I spent a great deal of time at the hospital to make sure our mother had the chance to eat and drink when she needed and receive the care that she needed. I tried to choose a new nursing home for her, but the opportunity for her to move slipped away for want of a Social Worker to supervise her move.

What do I think could have stopped the system failing Mum, and our family? And what do I think would help to stop this happening to others? My recommendation is to change the whole culture of how we deal with unsatisfactory care. Currently there is a reactive approach where we wait for the Care Quality

Commission to go in and audit the service (the care home, or nursing home or hospital) and then act if needed. We need to change this to a proactive approach. Here are some of my suggestions for moving in that direction:

- Staff should ask themselves, 'Would I want this done to my relative?'
- Staff should experience being a patient for a day on an older person's ward or as a resident in Older People's Services. The process should start with Directors, then Managers, then Ward Sisters, charge nurses, support staff and so on.
- Managers and staff should be enabled to accept criticism about poor practice in a positive way so that they think, 'What can I do about this to put it right?' rather than taking it out on the person who raised the concern.
- All staff, including volunteers, should receive training on what is poor practice, neglect or abuse and how to report these concerns.
- Trainers should empower learners by talking about what constitutes neglect and abuse and discussing ways to get help.
- Staff training should include who to raise concerns with (for example, when it is appropriate to follow an organisation's complaints procedure, or when they should contact the CQC or their local Healthwatch) and what to do if they are being bullied or victimised after making a complaint at work
- All paid staff should receive regular individual one-to-one supervision sessions.
- Limits on working hours should be reviewed. How can staff function if they are working a 14-hour shift?
- Older people receiving care in a care service, be it a nursing home, a care at home or a hospital, should be empowered by being given the knowledge as to what is good practice,

what is poor practice, what is neglect and abuse, and how they can do something about poor practice.

- Individuals in older people care services need to be empowered to talk about the place where they live and what they want via 'house meetings'.
- There should be easy-to-read posters in layman's terms, in eye-catching colours and in prominent places in care services, giving information (for example, 'If you are concerned about an older person receiving care this is who you should contact/what you should do...').
- All complaints procedures should be in a format individuals can follow, and should be easily accessible. (Having to ask reception or other staff for a copy is not good enough.)
- Something needs to be put in place to prevent the fear of reprisal whilst being a patient in a hospital bed or a resident receiving a service, such as an organisation they can telephone that will then let the hospital, home, etc, know that concern has been reported and they are watching out for that person.

I hope the people who can make these changes are listening.

Appendices

Choosing professional care

I have listed below the key issues to think about when choosing the professional help you may need. Remember that if you are in hospital and due for discharge, your needs will be assessed by the health and social care agencies and they will suggest what is right for you. Ask yourself:

- Exactly what help do I need?
- What is the best way to meet those needs?
- Do I need a care or nursing home that is staffed 24 hours a day?
- Would a care-at-home service, where I stay living in my own home and have carers come to help me, be best?

You do not have to do as the health and social care agencies advise. There are many alternatives and the health and social care agencies will be able to tell you about them. They include 'personal budgets', care at home, and various types of residential care. I have listed below some helpful pointers to asking the questions that will help you make your decision.

Personal budgets

Personal budgets are part of a new way of managing care and

support, called 'personalisation', which is designed to make sure the help you receive suits you as an individual. See the following on the Age UK website:

www.ageuk.org.uk/home-and-care/self-directed-support-direct-payments-personal-budgets-and-individual-budgets/

Care at home

To get a care assessment, contact Social Services and tell them you need some help to live in your own home. They will do an assessment which will include whether you need, for example, meals to be delivered, or adaptations to your home, such as bath rails, mobile hoists, or ramps for wheelchairs.

(If you need help with your house, shopping and/or garden you could contact your local Age UK shop or office.)

Identifying possible care or nursing homes

There are care homes with nursing care and care homes without. Both care and nursing homes provide 24-hour care.

At present there is no single authoritative source of up-to-date information. The Care Quality Commission inspects and regulates adult services and you can find reports on their website (www.cqc.org.uk). However, their inspection reports may be of inspections that have happened some months or years ago.

It is important to be aware that no care or nursing home will be exactly like where you are currently living.

Your doctor, or a social worker, may be able to recommend a care or nursing home. They will give you their professional opinion, but bear in mind that they only go in to visit, they are not there in the evenings, at nights or weekends, so cannot give an overview of the home.

You will need to consider:
• What level of support you need.

- What kind of room you are hoping to have. (For example, rooms with good views can be more expensive)
- Look at the websites and/or brochures for the homes you are considering.
- What do the possible homes offer in terms of personal care (can you choose if a man or a woman provides this), activities, trips out, chiropody, hairdressing etc?
- Find out what the charges are, and what services are included in these. (Beware of hidden extras.)
- Ask for a copy of the standard contract and also how payments should be made and when prices will be reviewed.
- Find out if there is a trial period and how long that is.

Visiting possible care or nursing homes

It is important always to take a look at several homes, if possible, before making a decision.

- For a first visit, ring the home and make arrangements to visit in advance.
- Do not go by first impressions alone.
- Speak to people who live there and staff who work there (out of ear-shot of the manager if possible to get people's true opinions).
- Try to go just before a meal time to see how this is managed and what the food might be like.
- If you think a home is possible, a second visit may be a good idea. For this, I would say with my 'professional' hat on, ring first as they will be busy; however, with my 'daughter' hat on I would advise turning up unannounced. If it's not convenient then the staff can explain why. You will get a better picture by just turning up.

Location

It's important to find a home that is in a convenient location for the things that are important to you.

- Is the home on a local bus route?
- How close is it to family members?
- Is it close enough for family and friends to visit?
- What is car parking like?
- How close is the home to the GP surgery?
- Will you have to change your GP?
- Will you have to change your dentist?
- How close is the home to the nearest hospital?
- Is it in a relatively safe area?
- Is the home or the area it is in noisy?

Environment – what the home is like to be in

You must also think about what will make the home pleasant, or not, to live in.

- Is the home clean?
- Is it warm?
- Are there any unpleasant smells?
- Is it well maintained?
- Are there railings and grab bars (around the home and in the bathroom and toilet)?
- If you may need hoisting, are hoists available and will you be measured for your own sling?
- Is there a lift?
- Is there wheelchair access?
- How easy will it be for you to move around the home, from one room to another, etc?

Communal areas

In a home, you will be losing some of your autonomy by living with other people and by being dependent on professional care. When you look round a prospective home, you will have a chance to find out:

- Who chooses what TV programmes or radio stations to have

on in the lounge?

- Who chooses when to have the TV or the radio, or CD, on?
- Is the TV, radio or CD generally blaring out?
- What do the people who live in the home do to occupy themselves?
- Will you feel comfortable in the communal areas (lounge, dining room etc)?

Bedroom

Depending on the level of care you need, you may be spending a large proportion of your time in your bedroom. It is very important you are happy with it. Find out:

- Whether you can choose to have an upstairs or a downstairs room;
- Who can enter your bedroom and why;
- Whether you can have a key to your bedroom;
- Whether a family member can have a key to your bedroom;
- Whether bedrooms have en-suite toilets and bathrooms;
- Whether the room can be decorated to your choice;
- Whether you can bring your own furniture;
- Whether you can bring your own belongings.

Activities/hobbies/independence

The following are important questions with regard to your continuing to be as independent as possible and to keep any former interests or hobbies going despite the change in your accomodation:

- Will family be encouraged to visit? Are there set visiting times?
- Does the home have an activities co-ordinator? (When you visit a home, see if there are any activities going on.)
- Will you be able to continue with your current hobbies? Will you receive help and support with this if you need it?
- How often will you be able to go out for walks? Or go into the garden?

- Are there any physical activities, such as exercise sessions?
- Will you be able to join activities when you want to? And when you do not want to, will this be respected?
- Does the home do trips out to the library? Or does a mobile one visit?
- Will you be able to have food and snacks when you like or will it have to be at designated times that suit the home?
- Do residents have to go to their bedroom in the evening at a time that suits the home? If the answer is 'yes', how early does this happen?
- Can you do your own washing and/or cooking?
- Can you still be responsible for taking your medicine/tablets?
- What happens to your money?
- Is there good mobile phone reception? Is there a private telephone either in your bedroom or somewhere within the home?
- Is there a computer you can use to send emails, access the internet, use SKYPE, and write letters to family and friends, available within the home? Will staff help you if you need assistance with any of these?
- If you use a wheelchair only for getting around, how often will you be hoisted from your wheelchair/a different chair/bed etc?
- When taking a bath, will you be able to soak in private once staff have helped you with the areas you cannot wash yourself any more?

Staff

Staff members may all be good, well-intentioned people, but if there are not enough of them, or if they have not had enough training, problems may arise. Ask:

- How many care staff and/or nurses are there compared with the number of people being cared for?
- How many staff are trained in Dementia, Medication

Management, Health and Safety, Dignity in Care?
- What is staff turnover like? Do they stay for the long term?
- How will the staff get to know you before you move in?
- Will you be provided with a buddy [staff member or an individual who lives there] to show you the ropes, help you find your way around the place, and settle in?

Your ongoing needs
Other questions that are important to explore include:
- What does the home do to prevent falls?
- What does the home do to prevent pressure sores?
- If you have a hospital or doctor's appointment will staff accompany you (if you need support)?
- What sort of transport will be available? Will you need to pay for this?
- What will happen if your needs change?
- How will the home let friends and family know if you are ill?
- Do other people at the home have the same needs as you?
- If you are not an English speaker, or if English is not your first language, are there members of staff and people who live there who speak your language?
- If you are an English speaker, are there members of staff who speak English?
- Will you be encouraged to give feedback on your care and other aspects of the home?
- Will there be regular residents' meetings where you can sit together and discuss issues, trips you want arranged etc?
- Is there access to advocacy services?
- What support is provided in relation to end-of-life care?
- Do you want/need someone to act on your behalf?

Further advice

A good place to start in looking for further advice is Saga. Their contact details are:

Saga Care Advice line: 0800 056 7996

Saga Respite for Carers Trust

Enbrook Park

Folkestone

Kent CT20 3SE

www.saga.co.uk/contact-us.aspx?tabid=health+and+care

Age Concern and **Help the Aged** have joined together and are now **Age UK**. Age UK provides information and advice about care, discrimination, computer courses and many other aspects. www.ageuk.org.uk

Carers UK provides advice and information to carers and the professionals who support carers, including:

- benefits and tax credits
- carers' employment rights
- carers' assessments
- the services available for carers
- how to complain effectively and challenge decisions.

http://www.carersuk.org/

Alzheimer's Society provides advice and information, including factsheets and a discussion forum for people with dementia and their carers.

http://alzheimers.org.uk/

How to comment on/complain about your care

'Complaints are important; when resolved they lead to improvement'
From www.spcconsultancy.com/abuse.html

The 'Friends and Family Test'

The new 'Friends and Family Test' is being rolled out to all GP practice patients, all acute hospital inpatients and A&E patients in England, and all users of maternity services, with a target completion date of December 2014. The test asks patients if they would recommend the NHS service they have used to friends and family if they needed similar care or treatment: www.nhs.uk/NHSEngland/AboutNHSservices/Pages/nhs-friends-and-family-test.aspx

Telling people face to face that you are not happy with something is not easy. To make it less difficult it is better to tell them what they have done well before telling them of your concerns, and ending with something else they have done well.

Put your concern(s) across in a non-threatening way and give the person time to digest the information. You also need to be aware of your body language. It is not a good idea to have your arms folded across your chest or your hands on your hips when complaining as this can appear to be aggressive and will aggravate the situation.

Throughout these past few years I have been surprised by how many people did not know they could complain about care services or hospitals, or thought they could not complain about nurses and doctors because they are professional people and it is something that you do not do, especially if you are a professional yourself.

How to complain formally about a care or nursing home

If you are dissatisfied with anything that happens in a care or nursing home you have a right to complain. You do not need to be living in the home to be able to do so. Anyone can raise a complaint – the person who lives in the home, a relative, a visitor, staff, members of the general public. The important thing is to report your complaint as soon as possible.

By law there should be a complaints procedure in place. All individuals being cared for in a home should be given a copy when they move in. Many homes have copies near to reception and you should be able to take one. If you cannot see any then you have the right to ask for one. This will tell you what you need to do and how your complaint will be dealt with.

You have a number of options. You can ask to see the manager and discuss your concerns or you can put them in writing. You can verbally tell the manager, but unless there is a witness to take notes, there is no proof that you have done this or record of what either of you said. Putting your concerns in writing provides a record and the manager should write back to you. However, it will depend on the nature of your concerns and the severity of them as to whether you choose to complain verbally or in writing.

If you choose to write, your letter should include:
- The name and address of the individual receiving care, the room in which they are/were staying and date(s) s/he was there;
- What you are complaining about: be very specific and re-member to include when and where the events in question took place;
- What you hope to achieve from the complaints process;
- The date of your letter.

Remember in addition to:
- Write your name and address on the back of the envelope or send it recorded delivery;
- Keep a copy of this and all other correspondence.

In the first instance, the complaint will be handled within the care or nursing home. If your concerns can be justified, your complaint should result in:

- An explanation for what happened;
- An apology;
- An indication of the steps that will be taken to review/improve performance.

If you are not satisfied with the outcome you can contact:

Your local Social Services office

Your local Healthwatch office

Age UK – www.ageuk.org.uk

Elderabuse – www.elderabuse.org.uk

The Care Quality Commission

CQC National Customer Service Centre

Citygate

Gallowgate

Newcastle upon Tyne

NE1 4PA

Telephone: 03000 616161

Fax: 03000 616171

How to complain formally about the NHS

If you are dissatisfied with any aspect of the care that you or a family member has received from the NHS, you have a right to complain. The first step is to visit or telephone the **Patient Advice and Liaison Services (PALS)**. They have a point of contact within each NHS Trust and they are able to advise patients and their families on how to make a complaint and reach an informal resolution. Or you can write a letter of complaint to the Complaints Manager. You can telephone, but then there will be no proof of what either of you said. Putting your concerns in writing gives proof that you made the complaint and the Complaints Manager should write back to you.

Your letter should include:

- The patient's name, address, name of ward and date s/he was there;
- What you are complaining about – be very specific, including when and where the events in question took place;
- What you hope to achieve from the complaints process;
- The date of your writing.

And remember to send it recorded delivery and to keep a copy.

Complaints should be made as soon as possible and certainly within 12 months of the event in question. Any NHS Trust has the discretion to extend the time limit depending on the circumstances of an individual case.

In the first instance, the complaint will be handled within the Trust, a process called 'local resolution'. If your complaint is justified, the process should result in:

- An explanation for what happened;
- An apology;
- An indication of the steps that will be taken to review/improve performance.

If you are not satisfied with the outcome of the local resolution process, you can contact the **Parliamentary and Health Service Ombudsman** (telephone: 0345 0154 033), who is independent of the NHS and the Government.

Alternatively, you can contact the Ombudsman for your part of the United Kingdom as follows:

- England: contact the **Local Government Ombudsman,** PO Box 4771, Coventry CV4 0EH, Telephone: 0300 061 0614 or 0845 602 1983;
- Scotland: contact the Scottish Public Services Ombudsman (for complaints about devolved national departments, including the NHS, prisons and universities, and local authority departments and agencies in Scotland);

- Wales: contact the Public Services Ombudsman for Wales (for complaints about devolved national departments including the NHS, and local authority departments and agencies in Wales);
- Northern Ireland: contact the Northern Ireland Ombudsman (for complaints about devolved national departments, including the NHS and universities, and local authority departments in Northern Ireland).

Complaints that are referred to the Ombudsman are known as 'Stage 2' complaints.

If you need help making a complaint then the following organisations can assist:

- **The Independent Complaints Advocacy Service (ICAS)**. They can help you make a formal complaint about NHS services by providing free and confidential advice and support.
- **The Citizens Advice Bureaux** and the **NHS** can also provide further information on NHS complaints.
- **Action Against Medical Accidents (AvMA)**. This is an independent charity which provides free specialist advice concerning NHS or private healthcare complaints where it is suspected that harm has been caused or there is a threat to patient safety.

Making a complaint at this level (local resolution) will not cost you anything and you do not need to involve a solicitor.

Seeking compensation

If you wish to apply for compensation, you are best contacting a solicitor. Some solicitors do a 30-minute free consultation to assess whether it is worth pursuing a case. If you are worried about the financial side of taking the NHS to court you can ask the solicitor if you are eligible for 'no win no fee'.

You must claim within three years of the incident/accident.

Freedom of Information Act 2000

If you would like or need information to support a case, you have to apply in writing to comply with the Data Protection Act 1998 and this can be done by email, letter or fax. It will depend on the information you want as to which website you need to apply for this information. For example, I wanted information on health and safety so I went on the Health and Safety Executive website and looked for the link 'Freedom of Information'. I clicked on it and after reading what I had to do (which was self-explanatory), I completed the form detailing what information I wanted and how I wanted to be contacted by them (by letter or email). I chose email so I could store the correspondence in a folder on my computer.

Please note that under Section 12 of the Act you can be refused the information if the cost of dealing with it exceeds £450 or the time required to retrieve it exceeds 2.5 working days.

Useful websites

NHS Service Search
At this website you can view comments left by others on their hospital, GP surgery, dentist, care home and at-home care. You can also rate these organisations yourself.
http://www.nhs.uk/NHSEngland/AboutNHSservices/Pages/nhs-friends-and-family-test.aspx

Action on Elder Abuse
Works to protect, and prevent the abuse of, vulnerable older adults.
www.elderabuse.org.uk

Age UK
Charity promoting the wellbeing of older people.

www.ageuk.org.uk
Telephone: 08001696565
For Age UK's guidance on raising concerns see:
www.ageuk.org.uk/Documents/EN-GB/Factsheets/FS59_
How_to_resolve_problems_and_make_a_complaint_about_so-
cial_care_fcs.pdf?dtrk=true

Alzheimer's Society
A great source of support, guidance and information for families and individuals living with and coping with Alzheimer's or
Dementia.
www.alzheimers.org.uk

Care Quality Commission
Inspects and reports on care services and councils and is independent but set up by Government to improve social care and
stamp out bad practice.
www.cqc.org.uk
For the CQC's essential standards of quality and safety:
www.cqc.org.uk/organisations-we-regulate/registering-first-
time/essential-standards

Department of Health
Providing health and social care policy, guidance and publica-
tions for NHS and social care professionals.
www.dh.gov.uk
For their guidance on the prevention of elder abuse see:
www.dh.gov.uk/prod_consum_dh/groups/dh_digitalassets/@
dh/@en/documents/digitalasset/dh_4074540.pdf
For the report *First national VOICES survey of bereaved people: key
findings report 20/9/12* see:
www.dh.gov.uk/health/files/2012/07/First-national-VOICES-
survey-of-bereaved-people-key-findings-report-final.pdf

Getting the most from your doctor
www.carewelluk.org/page/getting-most-from-gp-video

Healthwatch
'Healthwatch England is a national independent champion for consumers and users of health and social care in England.' It consists of a network of 152 local branches, with a central office providing leadership and support. By law, organisations involved in providing health and social care services have to listen to what Healthwatch has to say. Healthwatch works closely with the health and social care regulator, the Care Quality Commission (CQC) to ensure the voices of health and social care consumers are heard.
www.healthwatch.co.uk

National Institute for Health and Clinical Excellence
MidCity Place, 71 High Holborn, London, WC1V 6NA
www.nice.org.uk
For NICE quality standards for End of Life care:
www.nice.org.uk/nicemedia/live/13845/60321/60321.pdf

Saga
www.saga.co.uk
Saga Care Advice line: 0800 056 7996

Index

NOTES

NOTES